Arte Poetica

Que tu razón tenga un poco de parte.
Que puedas tomar el fuego primario,
esencialmente puro,
en la visión que asoma a un abismo interior y súbito,
donde después con tus manos
restaures, llama a llama,
la imagen de una rosa de fuego,
definible.

Angel Cuadra
1978

ANGEL CUADRA

The Poet in Socialist Cuba

Edited by
Warren Hampton

University Press of Florida
Gainesville/Tallahassee/Tampa/Boca Raton
Pensacola/Orlando/Miami/Jacksonville

The works by Angel Cuadra and Juana
Rosa Pita reproduced in this volume
appear by permission of the authors. The
translations titled This Man, Brief Letter to
Donald Walsh, and The Sadness that Overwhelms
Us are reprinted with the permission of
the translator, Catherine Rodríguez-
Nieto. The translation of "Writers in
Socialist Cuba" is reprinted with the
permission of Mark Falcoff. All
photographs are reproduced courtesy
of Angel Cuadra and Juana Rosa Pita.

The University Press of Florida is the
scholarly publishing agency for the State
University System of Florida, comprised
of Florida A&M University, Florida
Atlantic University, Florida International
University, Florida State University,
University of Central Florida, University
of Florida, University of North Florida,
University of South Florida, and
University of West Florida.

University Press of Florida
15 Northwest 15th Street
Gainesville, FL 32611

Library of Congress
Cataloging-in-Publication Data
Cuadra, Angel.
[Selections. 1994]
Angel Cuadra : the poet in socialist
Cuba / edited and with an introduction
by Warren Hampton.
p. cm.
Includes bibliographical references and
index.
ISBN 0-8130-1261-9 (alk. paper)
1. Cuadra, Angel. 2. Cuban poetry—
20th century—History and criticism.
3. Politics and literature—Cuba.
4. Cuba—Politics and government—
1959- 5. Authors, Cuban—20th
century—Biography. I. Hampton,
Warren. II. Title.
PQ7389.C84A6 1994
861—dc20
[B]   93-34678

In Memoriam

Carlos J. González Elcid

A Cuban gentleman and scholar.
Teacher, friend, and literary mentor
to Angel Cuadra and others of us
once upon a happier time in Havana.

This Man

*We will never know how many Cubans have lost their lives
in the sea, escaping from the island by way of the coast.*

There is a man moving through the night.
Perhaps no one will ever know about his small tragedy.
For days and weeks he has dreamed about this fear,
spent sleepless hours reviewing his terrors and his hopes.
He has smiled cordially,
pondered slogans, made political concessions
and secretly wrestled with his impotence.
He had to pass through those daily reefs, and so he did.
He was a simple man who went to the movies
and walked the streets under an ordinary name.
It's just that in him burned a light,
a very little light, painful, in his heart and temples.
He carried no weight in that sea
of great affairs where he was dragged
closer every day toward disaster.
And on this night, a night like any other,
this man shouldered his terrors and his hopes.

The moon, which is always mentioned in these cases,
revealed him on the coast,
and this man's light was shining out.
Every possible eye, every accusing finger
was raised in the darkness to denounce his flight.
In his solitude he had become a great man, a fugitive,
this simple man who did not leave his name,
and we will never know where
the ocean quenched his little light,
now that he has left the coast
where the winds sing through flutes of salt.

Angel Cuadra
Undated; translated by
Catherine Rodríguez-Nieto.

Contents

Introduction

As one-time "prisoner of conscience" and later "prisoner of the month" of Amnesty International, as well as the object of written homage by the intellectual community worldwide, poet Angel Cuadra Landrove is second in fame among Cuban political writers only to Armando Valladares, former political prisoner and author of the international best-seller *Contra toda esperanza* (translated into *Against All Hope*), an account of twenty-two years spent in Cuban political prisons from 1960 to 1982, when he was freed to go to France. The book describes the inhuman refinement of his torturers. It is a record of life and death in Cuban jails, among the best known La Cabaña, Isle of Pines, Boniato, and Combinado del Este, where Angel Cuadra also spent time and became, like Valladares, a *plantado* (a diehard) who chose near-nakedness over the uniform of a common criminal that the Cuban prison regime was forcing upon political prisoners.

But whereas Valladares became a poet in jail (*Desde mi silla de ruedas* [From my wheelchair]), using his unschooled verse to denounce Castro's gulags, Cuadra was already a recognized poet with international exposure when he was brought to trial for conspiracy and sentenced to a long prison term in 1967.

Born in Havana in 1931—he just missed being born in Tampa where his father, a cigar maker, had worked—Angel Cuadra was visited by the muse from the start. In kindergarten and the lower grades he delighted in memorizing children's verses and reciting them to his classmates. By age eight he was writing verses and keeping them in a notebook. His lifelong interest in the stage began with his participation in a schoolchildren's version of Snow White and the Seven Dwarfs. The basis of his literary training, however, began in earnest at age fourteen through his determined study of *la preceptiva*, the precepts of rhetoric and poetry imparted in Cuban secondary education, or *bachillerato*. Fusing talent, serious preparation, and inspiration, Cuadra precociously joined the rising Cuban literary generation of the 1950s, a highly productive decade in arts and letters albeit disastrous politically. Bowing to his working-class parents' yearnings, the youthful Cuadra enrolled as a law student at the University of Havana while also studying part-time at a business college.

In spite of a busy student existence, Cuadra found time to become captain of the University of Havana track team as well as to pursue his poetic and amateur stage interests. In 1954 he won a Martínez Villena prize at the University for his stirring *Canto de amor al Alma Mater* (Song of love to alma mater), done in Spanish alexandrine verse.

Typical of the university student body of the late 1940s and early 1950s was its inveterate opposition to the national government whether for real or imagined grievances, even when that government had been democratically elected. Corruption was the central issue; both opportunists like Fidel Castro and idealists like Angel Cuadra attacked it vigorously.

When former military strongman and ex-president (1940–44) Fulgencio Batista took the presidency through a military conspiracy in March 1952, the opportunists made their covert moves for future power. Leading from the rear, twenty-six-year-old Fidel Castro masterminded the 26 July 1953 attack on Moncada Barracks in Santiago de Cuba. Though rejecting violence for the moment, the university-centered intellectuals made common cause through civil opposition. By the time Angel Cuadra received his law degree early in 1956—Batista was to padlock the University a few months later due to student unrest—the stage was set for an anti-Batista urban underground split into terrorist and nonviolent factions. Meanwhile, paradoxically granted an amnesty by Batista in 1955, Fidel Castro repaid the favor by dis-

Angel Cuadra in 1959, wearing a Havana lawyers' pin.

embarking at the head of an armed insurrectionary band at the eastern end of the island in 1956, establishing his lair in the remote Sierra Maestra mountains while craftily awaiting events in Havana.

After 1956 Angel Cuadra led a double life, on the one hand that of a young lawyer, poet, and amateur theater director, while acting, on the other hand, as an anti-Batista conspirator loosely linked to the Revolutionary Student Directorate, Castro's 26th of July Revolutionary Movement, the Auténtico party, and other visible and invisible political opposition groups. In this political aspect of his life Cuadra's efforts make poignant reading. Still, it is the poet's literary persona that is historically noteworthy rather than his revolutionary activities in the late fifties and early sixties. The literary persona is the keystone of the trio of works presented here, although the two roles intertwined. In 1958, for instance, just as underground revolutionary activities escalated, Cuadra won a prize for his poem *Lamento a José Martí en su centenario* (A lament to José Martí in his centenary), awarded by the Circle of Iberian-American Poets and Writers of New York:

> Because you dreamed, Apostle, visionary dreams,
> the circular minute of the miracle.
> It was the voice of your blood and the blood of your word
> and the fragrant flower of your flank.

> Porque soñaste, Apóstol, de ensoñaciones puras,
> el minuto redondo del milagro.
> Fue la voz de tu sangre y la sangre de tu palabra
> y la fragante flor de tu costado.

Cuadra's place in the Cuban literary scene may be focused through the generational concept originally delineated by the Spanish philosopher Ortega y Gasset, in which each succeeding artistic and intellectual generation, born around the same years and experiencing a like environment, will either follow the same aesthetic direction of the previous one(s) or rebel and break off into its own opposing lines of creation. The generation that breaks with the past and creates its own direction becomes an avant-garde that eventually predominates. The short-lived Cuban republic (1902–59) included three such literary generations, with a fourth coming to life in the 1950s. Angel Cuadra was one of the latter's potential leaders; it was truly a lost generation, divided, fragmented, dispersed by the sovietization of the Cuban state after 1960. From their dispersal as a "school," some reached fame individually, among them the experimental novelist Severo Sarduy, an important contributor to the literary section of the short-lived *Lunes de Revolución*, now in self-imposed exile in France; the prize-winning novelist Lisandro Otero, a salient cultural figure and collaborator of the Cuban communist government to present times; the well-known poet and novelist Heberto Padilla, winner of a Cuban Union of Writers and Artists prize, who was forced by the Castro regime to recant in the egregious "Padilla case," now a professor at an American university; and Guillermo Cabrera Infante, now living in Great Britain, the first Cuban to successfully employ wordplay in the comic vein to capture the spoken word of a region or epoch, as he did in *Tres tristes tigres* (translated into *Three Trapped Tigers*), which mirrored Havana night life of the 1950s.

To grasp the vision of that upcoming literary generation of the fifties one must look back at the generation they chose to oppose, the third republican generation formed around seven literary reviews, not all of them of the same quality or duration. Starting around 1939, the most influential of these reviews by far was *Orígenes*, which also provided the rubric for the poets, artists, and writers grouped around it. After the early editorship of poet and painter Mariano Rodríguez and poet Alfredo Lozano, *Orígenes* was taken over by critic José Rodríguez Feo, its Maecenas, who for a time shared the editorship with the famed poet, novelist, essayist, and short story writer José Lezama Lima, author of the prize-winning, world-famous novel *Paradiso* (1974) and considered a preeminent figure in contemporary Hispanic-American literature.

Orígenes generally adhered to three main principles: first, art and poetry were viewed as transcending themselves to provide the observer and reader with a metaphysical interpretation of reality; second, art as an activity was to be free of social and political commentary; third, the artist was a unique member of society, providing the layman with new insights into himself and his cultural milieu. *Orígenes* rejected creole or nativist themes in fiction, socially committed literature, and folkloric writing. Besides accepting only original contributions from the supporting Cuban intellectual community, it turned its eyes toward Latin America and Europe, printing works by Vicente Aleixandre, Juan Ramón Jiménez, Louis Aragon, Octavio Paz, and others.

Coinciding with the ascendancy of left-wing poetry in Latin America, inspired by such poets as Pablo Neruda and the rise of anti-Franco poets of social protest in Spain, a number of young Cuban poets began to make themselves felt in the early fifties. Most of them opposed what they considered the abstract and abstruse art-for-art's-sake poetry of *Orígenes*, its evasion of reality with no stance on social and political problems, dehumanized and therefore powerless, in their view, as an instrument of change.

Angel Cuadra was not only a voice in the rising tide of opposition to *Orígenes* but also an organizer, cofounding with like-minded friends the poetic and literary group Renuevo, who launched their own poetry and manifestoes in favor of a more humanized, socially conscious poetry in everyday language. We shall infer that Renuevo received its energy as well from its members' opposition to the political corruption that continued unabated with the Fulgencio Batista regime and was made uglier by what to them seemed the increasing travesty of democracy that it represented. Several of those same members of Renuevo who remained in Cuba and were not dispersed, or assimilated into the Fidel Castro version of the Marxist state, later joined Cuadra in the anti-Castro underground poetry of resistance, Unidad Nacional Revolucionaria (National Revolutionary Unity), known by its acronym UNARE.

But, back in the first flush of Batista's downfall, upon the triumph of the Revolution on 1 January 1959, Angel Cuadra Landrove entered a brief period of literary recognition and popularity. His articles and poetry appeared in national newspapers and journals. He published his book of poetry, Peldaño. He became an international spokesman for the revolution and was translated into several languages. At the same time he became a government lawyer, which would turn out to be a helpful cover when he later agonizingly renewed his underground resistance activities, this time against his own revolution turned communist by Castro. Already months before the Bay of Pigs invasion by a CIA-trained Cuban brigade, a groundswell of resistance to the budding but not yet openly declared Communist takeover of the Cuban state was making itself felt by secret resistance groups, some of them armed, having no direct coordination with the coming invasion. Sabotage became rife. Aided by Soviet police advisers (even then) and surveillance techniques, the Castro secret police (G-2) tightened the screws. Thousands of suspects were rounded up throughout the island. Firing squads operated each dawn with grim regularity, most of their victims arbitrarily executed without benefit of trial—just a pointed finger. Still, the bombas kept exploding; the Castro regime tottered but held on. Then came the Bay of Pigs—a close one for Castro—and the defeat of the invading brigade. Though mostly unconnected to the event, the Cuban underground became demoralized and crumbled for the time being.

The definitive history of the secret-police reign of terror post-Bay of Pigs is still to be written. During that dark period when all seemed lost there remained stirrings of armed revolt and civil resistance. Underground journalism and poetry flourished. Though he was not alien to the armed resistance efforts, it was

through his clandestine intellectual involvement that Cuadra
was effectively snared after some four years of activity. He was
tried and sentenced to fifteen years' imprisonment. A curtain of
silence descended; he became a nonperson; his name and his
works disappeared from view in Orwellian fashion. His group's
poetry did circulate secretly, but under the pen names taken
when they were writing in UNARE. So by the time he left prison
a new generation had grown up knowing nothing of Cuadra or
the other poets of the fifties.

Even though Cuadra became a forgotten man nationally, he
continued writing poetry in prison. Some of it was rescued and
preserved, and published in *Impromptus* and *Tiempo del hombre*. *The
Sadness that Overwhelms Us* is a striking example of Cuadra's prison
poetry:

> The sadness that overwhelms us without warning,
> a gray ambush springing from God knows where;
> This bitterness that rises, absurd,
> in the midst of serenity,
> like a dark stain spreading
> from the entrails of a star;
> There has been no reason to suppress our smile,
> no previous disturbance in the coordinates of equilibrium.
> Yet we find ourselves, of a sudden,
> the unsuspecting recipients of calamity,
> stalked in a tangle of seismic fissures.
> Anguish cringes at the end of the hall.
> [*Translated by Catherine Rodríguez-Nieto (1985).*]

> Esa tristeza que nos inunda de súbito
> como un asalto gris que no sabemos dónde empieza.
> Esa sinrazón de la amargura
> en medio de la misma serenidad,
> como una mancha oscura que crece
> desde el vientre de la estrella.
> No ha habido causa para suprimir la sonrisa;
> no hubo antes trastornos en las coordenadas del equilibrio.

Pero allí nos hallamos de pronto
como destinatarios inocentes del mal,
acechado por las desordenadas grietas del sismo.
Se estrecha la angustia al final del pasillo.

Well into his prison sentence Angel Cuadra was contacted by
the expatriate Cuban poet Juana Rosa Pita, whom he had known
as a young girl:

I knew the fountain of the courtyard of your house:
green leaves would fall to the bottom
and a piece of sky would come down like the calm.
I, a visitor
welcomed by hands
that took care of you as a child.

As a youthful Renuevo poet Angel Cuadra often visited the
household where young Juana Rosa Pita was raised. Although
there was no significant contact between them, the memory of
the poet remained in Juana Rosa's mind when she emigrated.
After she blossomed abroad as a poet, Juana Rosa asked Cuadra
to read her poetry in 1976 through a mutual contact in Cuba who
visited Angel in jail.

In December of that same year, after serving ten of a fifteen-
year sentence, Cuadra was released conditionally. His freedom
did not last long. Forbidden to leave the country and with no
chance of publishing in Cuba, Cuadra risked having his prison
poetry mailed abroad to Juana Rosa. Published in the United
States, his book Impromptus cost the poet five more years in jail,
for the Castro dictatorship, instantly discovering the publication,
reincarcerated him to serve out the rest of his sentence.

After Cuadra's return to prison, Juana Rosa attempted to filter
her new poetry to Angel through one of his most intimate con-
tacts. Inexplicably, her correspondence was not passed on for
two years, as is revealed by the introductory letter in A Correspondence of Poems. Upon receiving her poetry, feeling certain he would
be punished for his international recognition by being cast into

solitary confinement in a distant prison—as indeed he was—
Angel set out to respond immediately to Juana Rosa's verses by
creating a poetic commentary in the time-honored Spanish tradition of the *glosa*, in which a passage or stanza of well-known
poetry is incorporated into the new poem and improvised upon
by the composer. In a way befitting its lyrical spirit, the poetry
presented here was smuggled out of prison in a musical instrument.

Owing to the intensity of their poetry in correspondence, a
platonic love doubtless developed between the two poets. But
time, separation, marriage, and the cares of everyday life took
their toll on the might-have-been-lovers. Still, these deeply lyrical verses are forever with us, frozen in time like the figures in
Keats' *Grecian Urn*.

My dear,
when you go about the world
with overcoat and hair,
with the exact brand of skin
and abstract papers that keep falling from your hands:
when you drop my name in the carelessness of a gesture,
and have to give explanations—
because they always ask for them—
concerning a mystery so simple
that it has no need for alphabets;
and they ask you about my face, which you don't know,
and about my character which you have known since birth,
because you bore it
in a birth of bread and tears . . .
don't utter, of the shadows of my iron bars, more than
     the sign,
don't speak of the vultures that scratch at me
for crumbs of hatred
and take light from the human clay;
speak to them of the poem that I defend
against a corrosion not from my iron bars, . . .

Poetry, more often than not, loses much in translation. But the feelings expressed in Cuadra's anisometric verses were masterfully conveyed to English by a peerless translator, the late distinguished Hispanist Donald D. Walsh, also translator of Neruda and Cardenal, among others. Unfortunately Donald Walsh was stricken with a long illness and passed away while Cuadra was serving out his time. Apprised of his faraway friend's illness, Angel wrote Walsh a letter-poem begging him to hold out till they could meet:

There are some men who crush my words,
tear me to pieces for producing beauty,
bring my poem to trial. . . .
But there are other men who rescue me
and save my poem like unransomed light,
who gather up its pieces of suffering clay
and, like Prometheus, lend me fire for it.
The fire of love, I proclaim it now,
that is the word I will defend
in the martyrdom, among the thorns. . . .
And you exist, Donald Walsh.
I knew nothing of your musical being,
of that gemstone clear and high, transparent.
Don't leave now
that I have found days dawning in my heart
that were sent me by your hand.
Don't leave now
that we begin to speak in a language
that unites the souls of Whitman and Martí. . . .
[Translated by Catherine Rodríguez-Nieto.]

The poem in its entirety is reproduced in this book at the end of *A Correspondence of Poems (from Jail)*. As to the latter, it has received attention in Europe. A German translation, *Korrespondenz in Gedichten aus dem Gefangnis*, by Franz Niedermayer, was published in 1981.

Coming after *Impromptus*, *Tiempo del hombre* (Time of man) was published in Madrid (Hispanova, 1977), containing poetry that led one critic to compare Cuadra's verses to the prison poetry of the Peruvian César Vallejo and the Spanish republican Miguel Hernández. Those two books alone, had he done little else, would have been enough to mark Cuadra as an outstanding dissident poet of the Castro era (see poet Pura del Prado's translated preface to *Tiempo del hombre* [1977] at the end of the book).

In 1976, having been able to get his entry sent abroad, Cuadra won a Venezuelan national prize for his martial poem *Ayacucho*. Later, in 1982, as he was about to serve out his prison time, he won the Pluma de Oro 1981 (Miami) prize. For three years, until 1985, he was not allowed to leave Cuba; he became an international *cause célèbre*.

The present edited volume includes three of Angel Cuadra's works in translation: the essay "Writers in Socialist Cuba," the collection *A Correspondence of Poems (from Jail)*, and selections from the 1963–64 UNARE underground essay, never published till now. The sequence begins with the most recent (1980s) and ends with the farthest back in time (1960s).

The first selection, "Writers in Socialist Cuba" (1985), is a monograph in Spanish funded by the Cuban-American Foundation, originally translated by Mark Falcoff, edited and revised for the present volume. Although it does not contain any of Cuadra's poetry and barely alludes to his work, it is a human-interest account of the poet's final three years in Cuba, of his attempt to adjust to the changes wrought upon his beloved Havana during his years in prison, of his meeting again with old friends and well-wishers and not-so-well-wishers. Curiously, Cuadra makes his narrative without a note of bitterness or sarcasm. He looks at the thought control and regimentation imposed by the Cuban authorities. He devises a classification of writers according to their degree of indifference, accommodation, or support of Communism—in his judgments Cuadra is evenhanded and tries to be fair. Lastly he relates meetings and discussions with youthful poets who know nothing of him and have never read a line of his verses. "Writers in Socialist Cuba" is a mosaic of Cuban intra-history of the later Castro years when all hope of a better life had evaporated and those of the old middle-class writers and artists who chose to stay or were not allowed to leave made the best of their lives under the circumstances, disappearing from the national intellectual and artistic life.

Because of financial limitations, *Poemas en correspondencia / A Correspondence of Poems* appeared in a low-cost bilingual paperback, very limited edition, in 1979. It deserves a wider audience, and here it is reproduced in its entirety, without editorial alteration, as the second selection from Angel Cuadra's literary production.

For our third selection we have chosen the lengthy UNARE historical-literary essay of 1963–64, prefacing a collection of poems condemning Castro-communist repression. The circulation of poetry against the regime had its genesis, first, in the Renuevo premise that poetry must reflect political and social realities and, secondly, in the (debatable) thesis that poetry could make a difference in national political life.

Along with other writings and poetry of heated protest, the UNARE essay circulated widely in Cuba, particularly in Havana. Its effect, however, was not measurable except perhaps to keep a counter-revolutionary conscience latent within the Cuban national psyche. But the Castro regime dug in with an ever-tightening grip, mounting a severe search-and-destroy hunt against all literary opposition, including the anonymous editor of UNARE—Cuadra himself—and its pseudonymous poets. Cuba's police state government eventually prevailed. When Cuadra was finally arrested for conspiracy, however, he appeared as a minor player, a mere intellectual opponent, not the head of an underground press, nor connected to groups with more violent determinations. Had the full truth transpired, the firing squad would have been his fate.

To understand early Cuban opposition efforts such as UNARE's, and their subsequent failure, one must go back to the fall of Batista. Little time elapsed after the January 1959 triumph of the Cuban revolution before it turned into a one-man show ominously marching toward Red fascism. With the passing of time a painful reappraisal dawned on the young revolutionary artists and writers who had participated in the original revolution for reformist democratic reasons. Now they beheld some unanticipated alternatives: accept body and soul Castro's thinly veiled pro-Communist line, escape into exile, or slip underground in opposition to a vigilant fanatical regime that still operated firing squads backed by a ubiquitous secret police.

Although a strong middle-class anti-Castro underground was in place well before the Bay of Pigs fiasco, the decision to join it on the part of former revolutionary Cuban intellectuals was hesitant and individual, precluding any concerted action ideologically; for the verbose Castro rhetoric, delivered over countless television hours, had mesmerized the Cuban public. Now anyone opposed to the *líder máximo* (maximum leader) was held to be at the very least a Batista sympathizer, anti-Cuban and a pro-Yankee imperialist to boot.

As pointed out previously, the defeat of the CIA-sponsored Bay of Pigs invasion collapsed the active arms collecting, bomb exploding anti-Castro underground which ironically operated independently of and was only loosely connected with the invasion. Indeed a claim is made by former underground survivors that they could have brought down Castro had it not been for the Bay of Pigs. Be that as it may, only a few heroic focuses of resistance were to remain in isolated areas like the Escambray and Oriente mountains under suicidally brave visionaries like the late Roberto Arias (see the poem in his name). Having learned his lesson in the Sierra Maestra, Fidel Castro took care to obliterate all resistance after his espousal of Communism, post–Bay of Pigs, massacring or moving off all peasants who may have lent support to the rebels.

It was in this disheartening environment that resistance to Castro was renewed. Activities were carried on by loosely con-

nected cells either dedicated to sabotage or to sending intel-
ligence abroad or to ideological agitation against the Communist newspeak. Thus was born UNARE, National Revolutionary
Unity, formulating an opposing national ideology to *fidelista* communism by establishing an underground press to distribute anti-
Castro literature; in fine, a Cuban *samizdat*.

Secretly a principal figure and ringleader of UNARE was the
government lawyer Angel Cuadra Landrove, already leading a
double life as an internationally translated poet of the Revolution. Under suspicion years before his arrest, the government
would not allow him to leave the country "to study abroad"; restricted to Cuba, Cuadra was given rope to hang himself while a
long game of cat and mouse ensued which lasted until the time
of his arrest and conviction in 1967.

What follows here are some translated portions of the clan-
destinely circulated 1963 UNARE essay-preface to a collection
of underground poetry against the Castro regime. The main
writer—it could not be told for years—was Cuadra himself.
The poetry included under the pen name of Alejandro Almanza
was his.

Before reading parts of this loosely translated essay, it would
be well to understand the reasons for both what is said and what
is left unsaid. Let us again consider the result of over four years of
fidelista rhetoric that vilified and discredited not only the former
Batista regime but also the entire Cuban Republic born under the
auspices of the United States in 1902. Against this brainwash of
the national psyche the writers of UNARE dared not suggest the
conservative (or radical) solution of returning to the old democratic republic and the constitution of 1940. In other words,
Castro-communist Pavlovian conditioning of the public obliged
UNARE to suggest the alternative of the idealistically conceived
New State (Estado Nuevo), a nationalistic counter to the Cuban
Marxist state. "If yesterday's dictators justified themselves in the
incapacity of our people for a democratic republican existence,"

announced the anonymous editor (Cuadra), "their heirs of today take communism as a pretext for their own perpetuation, appearing withal as saviors of democracy."

Another notable absence in the UNARE essay is any reference to the Church, now thoroughly discredited as an institution of an opprobrious past, an instrument of repression by the rich and privileged against the poor.

Receiving no favorable mention either is the United States, the object in those years of constant hate barrages by Castro. Perhaps the United States was a great place to emigrate to for all those secretly longing to leave the grey life of Communist Cuba, but Cubans knew, after the Bay of Pigs, that Uncle Sam was not to be trusted to pull their chestnuts out of the fire. Thus the UNARE essay takes on a nationalist fervor that is by inference tilted against the United States, particularly when it asserts that originally America wrested Cuban independence from the Cubans by its 1898 intervention, a curious corollary to the feeling already mentioned, that the Cubans alone would have gotten rid of Castro had it not been for American intervention through the 1961 Bay of Pigs episode. In this case Angel Cuadra's covert writings of that time simply mirror the 1963 Cuban zeitgeist.

Angel Cuadra was released from prison in 1982 after serving his full sentence. For three years, as already mentioned, he was not allowed to leave the island. The reminiscences of this interim are contained in his monograph "Writers in Socialist Cuba." When this restriction was lifted in 1985 he lectured briefly in West Germany and Sweden, whose ambassadors in Cuba, after appeals to Fidel Castro personally, secured his release. Soon afterwards Cuadra took up residence in Miami, where he joined the Cuban intellectual community in exile, writing a column for *Diario de las Américas*, participating in the Hispanic community's literary activities and also serving as an international jurist concerned with political prisoners worldwide.

Nor has Angel Cuadra neglected his basic poetic vocation. In 1988 he received a Spanish national award, the Amantes de Teruel prize, for his love poetry. In 1990, upon the reissuance of his ode *Requiem violento por Jan Palach*, in memory of the Czech martyr who immolated himself in Wenceslas Square, Prague, in protest of the Soviet invasion of 1968, he received special recognition from President Vaclav Havel of Czechoslovakia. In 1991, together with his sister Marta, a pianist and musicologist, Angel Cuadra created a lecture-recital exploring the connection between poetry and music from primitive times to the present.

                                                                 Warren Hampton

Writers in Socialist Cuba (1985)

Angel Cuadra

I

Havana has always been an exceptionally beautiful city. Like any metropolis rich in tradition, it is surmounted by a kind of halo one senses in its streets, its buildings, in its very atmosphere—as if one could penetrate through a poetic sixth sense, its very soul, whose praises so many have sung across the centuries.

After many years as a political prisoner, to return to Havana once more involves searching for that essence still lurking behind the many crumbling facades and omnipresent in spite of the city's generally impoverished aspect. I remembered one of the verses I composed in jail:

> The poem that I recited one
> long night in Havana
> surrounded by friends and by dreams
>
> el poema que dije en una
> noche abierta de la Habana
> con amigos y sueños

That simple, free-spirited Bohemia no longer exists: there are no more all-night cafés where people can engage in endless conversations. Which leads to the question, Where are the poets, the writers, the artists? What are they doing? How should we classify them? According to their circumstances and attitudes towards present-day socialist society, which sponsors its own "official"

Cuadra reciting his poem *Lamento a José Martí* on José Martí's birthday, 1955.

version of culture? Best to begin with the obvious: not all writers
and intellectuals in Cuba are opposed to the present political system, and not all favor it. More to the point, there are variations
and special circumstances that can only be evaluated through direct experience. In that sense, the anecdote is more useful than
any sociological explanation.

II

One afternoon—one of my first, actually, after my release from
prison—waiting my turn in line to pick up some photographs,
I heard someone call me by name. To my agreeable surprise it
was an old friend, a poet who during the 1950s had joined me in
several literary enterprises. We were no longer young but we still
had poetry in common.

In response to his invitation I later called on him at home—
which turned out to be a tiny corner of an old building cut
up into apartments in which many doors open out onto one
long hall. It was really a former commercial atrium across the
street from an old mansion. My friend's dwelling consisted of
two small rooms. On the upper level was a bedroom which he
himself had built at considerable cost and effort, connected by
means of a concrete staircase to a sitting room. This latter was a
motley saloon divided in two by means of some hanging mats
and a sofa. Next to the sofa was a lamp which made possible
nocturnal reading and writing. Behind the sofa was an improvised dining room—a small eating table and a 1950s refrigerator.
And in the front half, the part of the room that gave on to the
street, he added a large chair and another sort of sofa with small
pillows. There was hardly room to move around in. A bookcase
covered the entire right-hand wall, and the rest of the wall space
was covered with paintings, certificates and decorative objects.
Books, diplomas, paintings . . . logical relics of a past life pro-
ductively spent in the service of culture and art. A welcome if
humble environment, located in the old and now somewhat ne-

glected district of Luyanó, where during many an afternoon I
was left to find friendly counsel during days of great uncertainty,
a drink when needed, and a welcome discussion of poetry but
also of literary and human themes, as well as a useful analysis
of our own personal situations, and the cultural and political
situation of our country.

My friend was one of those writers that belongs in the first
category of our taxonomy: people who are completely isolated
and subsist at the farthest fringe from official cultural life. Having
dissented from the political choices adopted by the revolutionary government three years after its accession to power, the only
alternative was isolation: withdrawal from public intellectual life.
In effect, he had exiled himself to an interior world, to literary
life hidden from all but himself. He worked as a common laborer
in a factory, and after eight hours of exhausting toil he would return to his tiny home, put behind him the struggle for his daily
bread, stretch out on the sofa, and read, dream—even, at times,
write poetry, simply out of the natural need which any poet has
to versify—by the light of his tiny electric lamp. The latter was
his only source of illumination, so that, extinguished, his entire
domestic universe was thrown into a curious half-light. It occurred to me then (and still does now) that this situation was the
aptest metaphor of his spiritual existence.

This poet, divorced from the person he once was, lived upon
two illusions, or rather, compensations. "I have my son," he
said, "to whom I talk on the phone every day and who visits
me on weekends. And I have my poetry, which visits me from
time to time, though with less and less frequency. But it never
completely gives up on me."

The explanation for his voluntary isolation was easy to come
by—dissent with the regime. He explained to me that he had
decided that the best way to preserve his intellectual self-respect
was to refuse to write poetry which recognized limits or partook
of compromises whose purposes he did not share. Once, during
his long years of ostracism, he completed several research tasks

of a historical rather than literary nature—simply as a means of intellectual exercise. To find an outlet for his cultural loneliness, he spent long hours of his precious spare time studying the origins of his hometown, located north of Havana. In this study he suggested a bold hypothesis—which cast considerable doubt on notions popular with historians past and present, on the origins of the first towns founded in this part of the Province of Havana, and even, I should add, on the origins of Cuban aboriginals, the long since extinct Siboneys. Though he addressed his work to the Academy of Sciences on one occasion, and to the Historian of the City of Havana on another, no one paid him the slightest attention.

One day he paid a visit to his hometown, and at a local Protestant church he gave a completely unofficial lecture on the subject. As a result he was called and questioned by the local leadership of the communist party, to whom word had arrived that my friend was contradicting or misrepresenting history as officially accepted. I did not understand why he was so sure this was the reason why his valuable study failed to gain serious attention. He nearly became exasperated trying to convince me it was all because of what his statements contradicted. Besides, he as a poet had taken an active part in literature, in UNEAC [National Artists' and Writers' Union of Cuba, sanctioned by the regime] and its activities at the beginning of the Revolution. He had quit to remain isolated and silent, and that isolation and silence was tantamount to opposition to official culture. For that he had a price to pay.

At the time of my departure he was still trying to get his historical studies to be taken seriously in academic competitions. For this purpose he found it useful to make some, shall we say, opportune corrections to his work. (I even helped him.) "I have done this work so that I shall not die completely," he said, "but I shall not bring out my poetry again." When I suggested that perhaps someday some of his verses might again find publication, he assured me that this was impossible. Were he to be published

abroad, he ran the risk of problems in Cuba. Moreover, he had
no intention of ever leaving the country; to publish at home—
where every word had to pass muster with the censors—was impossible without reentering the very circles he had voluntarily
departed so many years ago. "But the poet," he kept repeating
to me, "always is ready to begin life anew. And if things were to
change . . ."

(When I finished this essay, I learned that my poet friend had
since died. His neighbors found him after two days of not re-
sponding to knocks at his door. There he was, on the sofa of
his tiny salon, under his lamp, surrounded by the books, paintings and articles that kept him company in his lonely years of
voluntary exile, possibly having received his last visit from the
muse. Now that he is no more, I can name him: Angel N. Pou,
cofounder of the Renuevo Group in 1957, author of *Cantos de Sol
y Salitre* and *Una Brizna en el Oleaje*, besides many other unpub-
lished works, conceived in half-light and silence, works which
unfortunately will never be published.)

III

Some of the points I have just made with respect to Pou remind
me of personal experiences with two other poets, one some
years before my incarceration.

It seems to me that it was around 1964: I had a meeting with
Eliseo Diego and Octavio Smith, both of whom belonged to
the Orígenes Group. The place was the 1830 Restaurant in the
Vedado district, at the mouth of the Almendares River in Havana.
Both were practicing Catholic poets, extremely pleasant per-
sons, who wanted me to help them produce a theatrical offering
with some religious sections which they proposed to mount at
the parish house in Calabazar, a small town south of the capital. Once we had worked out the business details which were
the ostensible purpose of our lunch, we turned to a discussion
of poetry. Both were on the verge of publishing collections of

verse. I found it odd, I said, that as both of them were Catholics, the UNEAC was going to publish their works without difficulty, since neither contained revolutionary or social themes, and even more, since neither was connected in any way to the new literary establishment. Eliseo explained to me that he had been offered publication without any such conditions. I suggested to him that it was difficult to imagine that a great poet, and above all, a distinguished intellectual like himself, might not be asked to participate or cooperate in some form or another, after a favor of that magnitude. He replied to me again that no one asked him anything in return. I could not help warning him, however, that precisely because they did not demand that he write in favor of the Revolution or on one or another particular theme, he could expect that—given his good name and his intellectual credit— he would soon be asked to become a member of some literary prize jury mounted by the UNEAC, and that he would find it difficult to say no. And that would just be the beginning.

When we parted—after working out the details for the production of his play—I left reproaching myself, musing that perhaps (because of my long history of underground conspiratorial activities, about which they knew nothing), I was too prejudiced and extreme, and that more than likely, since Eliseo was a convinced practicing Catholic, they would ask nothing of him in exchange. Maybe one book by a poet of unquestionable quality such as he, figuring among the list of official titles, would be a sufficient political contribution to the Revolution's cultural programs.

Time passed. In those days I took classes at the Alliance Française, less than two blocks away from the Writers' Union. One afternoon I made a rare visit to the latter to have a drink in the cafeteria, which was open to the public. Leaving the door of the garden that issues out onto 17th Street in Vedado, I accidentally bumped into someone who was entering and who, as a result of our collision, dropped the papers he was carrying. While I apologized and hastened to try to help him gather up his materials, I noticed it was Eliseo. When I asked him what he was doing there, he answered in his characteristic humble yet cordial way, "I've come to hand out the awards in a contest on whose prize jury I have served." I smiled and we parted amicably.

In subsequent years this poet, who continues to be a practicing Catholic and as good a writer as ever, has continued to lend his paradoxical and active support to the organisms of official culture in Cuba (such as the Union of Writers). This is so not because the latter publishes his poems, which would be less remarkable, and even, in the final instance, understandable, but because he has gone so much farther than one would have thought necessary, particularly in a man of deep religious convictions. The last thing I read about him in Cuba was an interview in which he said that one of the greatest experiences of his life was to visit the Soviet Union, which he praised in extravagant terms. When I read this in Cuba, having recently emerged from prison, cut off for many years from present-day Cuban society in all of its extension, all kinds of questions occurred to me. One was, is it not possible some people simply cannot avoid participation in life around them? And might it not be true that between this and the total oblivion of intellectual death through silence (such as experienced by the first poet I have spoken of) there is no third option? After all, not everybody feels able to emigrate, or is even able to under all circumstances. With regard to the case of a Catholic poet who functions within the Marxist cultural milieu, what particular mission, I thought, does he imagine he is fulfilling between two poles so utterly opposed one to the other?

One night, more or less around the same time of the previous anecdote, wandering along the streets of Vedado, I ran into a poet of my generation whose name I shall have to omit here (as I shall in other cases in the course of this essay) to save him from any possible difficulties. This man was a colleague both in the professional and poetic sense who, like me, had made a conscious decision to distance himself from official cultural activities. That night, having not seen me for quite some time, he spoke with a mixture of disenchantment and self-justification. He told me he had decided to publish some ten-line poems, *décimas*, to be precise. They had offered him the opportunity. Since he could not leave the country, he argued, and since as a poet it seemed useless to sacrifice his vocation by remaining silent, and so on, he concluded with a question that I suppose was intended to overcome any possible objection, "What, after all, can a poet do with silence in the Soviet Union, for example?"

Twenty years later, subsequent to my release from prison, I had further news of him. He had a nervous breakdown and no longer wrote poetry. He now worked in one of the official cultural organisms whose name I have forgotten; at times he takes part in some of its collateral activities.

As it happens, because he was in charge of some meeting or lecture, I had further news of his existence. I did not attend the particular function in question, but in Cuba one always hears something about them. Then—a still more surprising coincidence—I met up with him again, not face to face, as it were, but as part of an impersonal public at another such function. Afterwards we greeted each other and spoke briefly. I do not know if he was aware of my political situation—I suppose so, although it didn't come up—but, in the fashion of someone slightly distracted (his current pose), he spoke to me with cordiality, completely free of the burden of self-justification which so heavily characterized our previous conversation. I recalled the incident because he told me that he was going to publish some *décima* poems. I could not imagine, save in the theater of the absurd, that they were the same of which he had spoken nearly twenty years before, on that avenue in the Vedado district of Havana, an exchange which had so overwhelmed me with its sinister significance.

IV

The previous two examples aid us in considering the other group of writers and poets in Cuba, those who operate within the

Angel Cuadra visiting famous Cuban singer Celia Cruz in Madrid,
1988, when he received the Amantes de Teruel poetry prize.

sphere of official culture, whose works are published frequently,
who participate in government functions and ceremonies, who
figure as "revolutionaries" and are presented to the world as sup-
porters of the government and communicants of its ideology,
which is to say, writers "integrated" into the revolutionary process. But it would be inadvisable to lump so many people under
one generalized rubric; among the ranks there are many different
cases and situations, each requiring its own separate explanation. Each one would have to be classified by his or her personal
circumstances. Let us, then, allow the anecdote to be the proper
organizing principle.

V

Gradually, like someone returning from a lengthy journey, I cau-
tiously drew near my beloved ancient city of Havana, to its beautiful physical essence and to its even more delicate social and

cultural persona. I approached it with care, by means of brief, tentative sorties, surveying the terrain before actually entering it. I wanted to avoid disagreeable incidents, meeting or even brushing up against anyone belonging to the stage army of extremist intellectuals (generally mediocre, and for that very reason, extremist) who might purposely provoke a hostile or intemperate reaction on my part. Obviously, given my situation, this was the last thing I wanted; after all, I was not merely a former political prisoner but a writer as well, an intellectual (as we style it) who before 1959 and in the early days of the revolutionary process played a certain cultural role; thereafter I was known to many Cuban intellectuals, including those who today grasp the reins of the official culture.

When one returns to the streets of Cuba after long years of confinement, cut off from a national life which has changed so much, one feels odd, a bit like a foreigner visiting one's own country. Initially one knows—or imagines—he is being watched. He moves somewhat tentatively through streets many of whose names have been changed. The bus lines are not the same as before; the routes have different numbers and go to different destinations. One finds oneself avoiding especially the centers where large crowds tend to gather—especially popular recreational areas like the "pilot beer gardens" (which I visited once out of sheer curiosity), carnivals, fiestas, even the corner of 23rd and L Streets in Vedado, site of the popular and well-known Coppelia ice cream garden. (It seems to be frequented by certain doubtful social elements and therefore subject to periodic "sweeps" by the police, although I know this to be the case only by hearsay.)

But in cultural circles the problem is a bit more subtle. It is there that my caution is best advised, all the more so because during my first days of freedom I ran into the poet Adolfo Suárez. The encounter took place at a bus stop in the Santos Suárez district. We boarded the vehicle together. The initiative was his. Extending his hand he dryly remarked, "So you're out now? That's good." And then, "So you've finally come to understand us?" By now we were being crushed by an overflow of passengers. "Understand in what sense, old boy?" I asked, a bit angrily. I saw that he was a bit upset. And while he went on trying to explain what he had in mind, I recalled that in 1958, out of motives of affection and respect I had taken him to a meeting of the Renuevo literary group, in whose final anthology he eventually appeared. He was young and eccentric at the time (perhaps he still is a bit odd) and had nothing whatever to do with Marxism. "You'd better understand," I said, interrupting his rambling explanation, "I am the same person you always knew, I haven't changed at all." Then he tried to smooth matters over by saying, "Well, I'm the same too, only different." With that remark, which he did not attempt to explain, the conversation ended. (Nonetheless, I should say that sometime later, at the Havana Book Fair, at an open air reading by poets from Matanzas, Adolfo came up to me, this time showing evident affection, as if—I imagined—to cancel out the bitter taste of our previous meeting.) Latterly, whenever I ran into him he was always cordial. With this first experience with a Cuban intellectual during my initial period of freedom, I had even more reason to approach the cultural world of Havana with caution and a certain wariness.

I owe much to the generosity of a good friend, another former political prisoner, for pulling me out of the ostracism of those first three years of freedom. Without him I would never have been able to make my first tentative approaches to the cultural environment of Havana. There I became acquainted or reacquainted with people, discovering who was who and reconstructing my outdated image of the world I had left behind.

My friend is a professional who, returning to society after years of prison, is expressly prohibited from practicing his calling. He must earn his living through hard manual labor; he dedicates what free time he has to attending lectures or conferences on historical or cultural subjects of the many offered in Havana, usually free of charge. I went with him to a series of lectures at the National Library on the arts of antiquity, to another on the work of Cirilo Villaverde, especially his Cecilia Valdés, at the very time when a polemical film based on that novel was being released. (The film in question twisted the original almost beyond recognition, nonetheless becoming a cause célèbre in Havana cultural circles.) With him, too, I went to a series on "Colonial Havana, Its Buildings and Their History," at the Amphitheater, a cycle complemented by Saturday tours of the sites under reconstruction thanks to the admirable support of UNESCO. And I also attended lectures on colonial architecture and sculpture, sponsored by the Cuban National Trust in the patio of its headquarters near the docks in Old Havana. In all of these activities, I saw once again—this time from a distance—some of the established figures of Cuban culture, as well as younger people researching some extremely recondite subjects. I wandered along marvelous cobblestoned streets, among old buildings from the colonial period, alongside my friend and a group of like-minded souls. It was common at the conclusion of any of these functions to see groups of elderly people clustering around, people who loved anything old or historical, in this case the stones of old Havana, which provided a momentary flight from the present as well as a link—at once paradoxical and necessary—between the past and a present which is difficult to understand and explain.

Two kinds of testimony brought me up-to-date on the Cuban cultural scene: stories told me at second hand and those related by the actors themselves, those I could draw away from the group.

"What happened to Lezama Lima?" I asked someone. I never particularly cared for his work; it failed to speak to me in the way it spoke to so many poets of my generation. Quite the contrary: at the end of the 1950s some of us—all just starting out—favored moving away from poetry which was inaccessible to ordinary people. It was not a question of denying the value of Lezama Lima's work; we simply felt he had fulfilled his mission and must now step aside for a new, more resonant form of expression which the times now approaching would require, which was another way of saying that from now on art would be judged by its social function. Thus it was natural that poets of my generation—all having passed through and gone beyond Lezama Lima and his circle—should take charge of official culture in the immediate postinsurrectionary period. We turned our backs on the style in which we had been schooled and put in its place a new poetry of slogans to carry to the masses (whose own means of expression were not yet sufficiently evolved). The recondite and abstruse gave way to a crude colloquialism of speech into which Cuban poetry has subsequently been frozen.

This being the case, it can be imagined how shocked and even confused I was by the appointment of Lezama Lima to the vice presidency of the Writers' Union in the 1960s. In that capacity his signature appeared on numerous official declarations of the Union, among them a cheap shot at the Chilean poet Pablo Neruda for attending a meeting of the PEN Club in New York; although it is known that the decision was not Lima's own; nor many other positions he was forced to take whenever political considerations so required. With the passing of time I have learned to be less critical of Lezama. In prison I read his novel *Paradiso*. And after going through several more of his books, I eventually decided that he, at least, was faithful to his art, even though, given his position at the Writers' Union, he was always presented as one of the Cuban writers faithful to the Revolution and its government. He was used—his fame, his prestige, his following extended far beyond Cuba's borders. But he also used the vehicles of the Revolution for his own work. (Sometime later I was told that Lezama himself had once remarked that this was the way he was able to get *Paradiso* published in the first place!) When he no longer adequately served purposes unclear to me, he then fell into disgrace, perhaps all the more quickly because his case followed that of the poet Heberto Padilla. They told me Lima spent his final years under virtual house arrest, forbidden to accept any of the many invitations he received from abroad. He died in the loneliness of a pall cast upon him at the last moment, even though that pall no longer had any effect internationally.

Even more lamentable is the case of Virgilio Piñera, one of the greatest Cuban playwrights. He was furthermore a novelist, short-story writer and poet as well as a member of the old writers' group Orígenes. Virgilio died in 1979. I found out by word of mouth from artistic circles I frequented that he spent many years until his death in a lamentable isolation at home.

I cannot recall Piñera's ever having been officially praised as a revolutionary partisan. I do indeed remember him in 1960, the only time I saw him, when I attended the First Meeting of Writers and Artists, in the city of Camagüey. He appeared diffident, politically indifferent and even irritated at certain manifestations of irrelevant "moralism" made by both [Nicolás] Guillén and the Spanish [Republican] ex-general Bayo. I now found out he was once arrested but freed in a few days through the efforts of revolutionary friends. It left him with a residual panic he never lost. For years his work, unrelated to the Revolution, was silenced. I was told he felt harassed, with no role whatever in Cuban cultural life.

Those who knew him well and visited him in his internal exile knew he continued to write; his talent required an outlet even though he knew there was no possibility of ever seeing his work published. Piñera thus belongs to the category I devised to describe my poet friend at the beginning of this essay, among those who are completely isolated and exist at the farthest fringe away from official cultural life. With Piñera's death a valuable work may have been lost (because it will not see the light of publication). At any rate, those who were able to read parts of it have assured me that it was as good or better than his earlier known work.

I should point out, however, some years after his death, probably in 1984, I saw on Havana television his well-known play *Aire frío*. The question came to my mind, could there be posthumous rehabilitation of the person and the works of this writer? It is worthy of note, of course, that *Aire frío* is the dramatization of the problems and vicissitudes of a lower middle-class Cuban family just prior to the triumph of the Revolution, if one should wish to present a critical view of prerevolutionary society. But now, as to Piñera's later works, those that we know not but which might have contained contradictory material at odds with official cultural policy, could they possibly be saved in that foreseeable recovery? One can only speculate. But it may indeed serve the larger interests of Cuban cultural policy to do just that.

VI

Within the category of fringe writers—that is, those who work in silence, fully aware that their books can never see the light of day—I came to know not merely those who belonged to older generations, but to younger ones as well. One night at a lecture a friend introduced me to a young poet who had heard about me and expressed a desire to meet me. He was only eighteen years old and did not live in Havana but periodically came to town to visit relatives. We met at the door of the Lyceum of Old Havana, together with a cousin and a friend of the cousin, both about the same age. The cousin was, in fact, an arts graduate. It was towards the end of 1984. This young poet, incredibly mature and intelligent, appeared to be at least twenty-three or twenty-four years old, and when he spoke, older still. He began by expressing admiration for me, but by the end of the meeting I was the one who was doing the admiring. I insisted that he never tell me his full name, a practice I always applied in such cases, perhaps a persistent remnant of my past as a conspirator.

This young man explained to me why he did not belong to the literary workshop in his town. After explaining to me its rules, he asserted that he, for one, was not ready to have his poems or short stories analyzed by a collective where some members could excise elements at will and others add to them; or to decide whether one particular reference was too obscure and therefore incompatible with the photographic realism dictated by artistic policy generally; or to determine if some other expression was reminiscent of discredited bourgeois art. He added that the fact that such alterations were suggested rather than ordered—he was under no particular obligation to accept them—was irrelevant. To the degree that they existed at all, they inhibited a writer, they forced him one way or the other to compromise his craft. Such a situation was intolerable to him.

For a moment I privately despaired at his literary future, for to cling to such views, particularly when he expressed no intention to emigrate, amounted to casting his poetic work into darkness and silence. No one would ever know of him or his work, so that he would lack the stimulus needed to develop further. He expressed no intention of publishing abroad. Nor did I suggest it; given the risks involved, I would not have wished to assume the responsibility. He did not believe it possible to win one of the periodic literary competitions, because his subject matter, he told me, would not fit within the approved artistic parameters. I tried to argue with him, but he showed me a newspaper clipping (which he let me keep) which reported a contest in some provincial Cuban town in the genre of love poetry. Among other things, the participants were required to establish their "revolutionary integration" and to submit their work under their own name. The article eloquently canceled any possible further argument I might make even though I insisted (and I still believe) that there are bound to exist somewhere in the country less rigorous requirements for competitions of this sort.

In order to hear his poems we decided to go to the home of his cousin's friend, for since he lived alone, we would be more secure (or feel as if we were). On the way, in the bus, I reflected upon how things had changed, recalling how almost eight years before, a few days after leaving prison, I visited some young writers who again completely outside the official culture wrote works which were also out of line with the prevailing aesthetic. They gathered periodically in a house in one of the Havana suburbs, quite openly and with no attempt at dissimulation. Their works did not attack the political system, at least ostensibly, but rather commented upon it obliquely. The group was eventually repressed, and one of the members, for having circulated his work among his friends, was tried and sentenced; today he lives in exile.

At last we reached the friend's house—there were only a few of us—and behind closed doors we listened to the young man's poems. They seemed to me of genuine quality, written in the accepted colloquial style. While some were political, the majority were not. But in all of them a genuine glow of future poetic promise was evident, a broad, timeless vision unblemished by sectarianism or resentment. This, I thought to myself, is the way dissident or fringe poetry gets read nowadays. It no longer circulates at all, at least as far as I knew. Instead it is read aloud to trusted groups of friends. It lives on only in the memory of those who hear it, comforted by the assumption that at the same time somewhere else others are listening to yet other prohibited works, the communion service of a forbidden rite.

Nowadays I often think about that young poet. I wonder if in the future he will come to constitute part of that group of writers who lead an isolated existence, in the half-light and silence, his works never destined to circulate, just as in the case of those others I have already described. Or will he take the other path, plunging his present work to the bottom of some secret file drawer, to enter the country's public intellectual life, where at least he will be able to survive as a writer and a figure in the literary history of the society where he lives and where he will eventually die?

VII

The literary workshops in Cuba are set up to service new writers or those who have a particular interest in literature. There people are taught technique, a bit of the canon, and of course theories of literary art as understood by Marxist ideology. At these

workshops the practical exercises include collective delibera-
tion; poems and stories are subject to group analysis. But in Cuba
there are also "informal groups" (*peñas libres*) in which, as the
name implies, no prior membership in a literary workshop is
required; one need only be invited by one of the habitués. At
least that was the case in the group I attended in my old neighborhood, now known as the "10th of October" district. I believe
that, except for the person who invited me, no one there was
aware of my political past. I knew none of the people save for
two or three decrepit poets who wrote in a decadent démodé
style and who had never attained any fame or distinction. Perhaps I had known them some thirty years before, but only in the
most superficial way. As far as they were concerned I could have
spent all the intervening years in my professional calling; they
made no attempt to find out. At the group they read their poems,
as did their younger colleagues. The air sparkled with witticisms
and bons mots. There was much "I'll read you if you'll read me," an
old joke among poets.

But what interested me about that particular night (I attended
another one subsequently) was that it featured a very young
woman, the product of a literary workshop, who was going to
read her poems. I listened carefully to that talented, beautiful
twenty-year-old as she read her verses written in the colloquial
speech which is the obligatory poetic style in Cuba. More than
once she referred to her "teacher" (she spoke his name) prior to
reciting a poem. Her verses were all workmanlike. Some were
quite good. The themes were personal, several were love poems.
All of them showed evidence of a genuine link between senti-
ment and expression. I had the same sense when she read her
few political poems, all of them of revolutionary orientation, to
be sure.

She was a poet belonging to the latest budding Cuban literary
generation, the same one as our young nonintegrated poet of the
previous anecdote. But they did not belong to the same political
outlook. She could rise, if she held to her same outlook, and

would be able to join in latterday Cuban literary and cultural publications; she would exist for "our" literature. He, by holding on to his attitude would not be part of the literary anthologies; he would not exist for "our" literature.

This melancholy reflection occurred to me that night, as I left the gathering, while strolling along the 10th of October Boulevard where many years ago, at the same age as those young poets of today, I used to recite my poetry among my friends, in poetic throngs under the auspices of no one, improvised on street corners and in the cafés of the old avenue of my *barrio*.

VIII

In this cautious approach to Cuban cultural life during my first three years of freedom, my most deliberate—my most dangerous—decision was to attend a public meeting at the UNEAC at its headquarters in Vedado. The occasion was a lecture by a foreign intellectual. The subject was of great interest to me, so I decided to risk it, knowing full well, I confess, that I was bound to run into people I used to know, the executives of the Union, and perhaps even an extremist who would make a scene about my presence. Hence I made a decision before going that I would not speak to anyone who did not take the first step and greet me first.

In the patio of the Union's building small groups of people were talking while waiting for the hall to open. I recognized a few of them. Some I could recall by name, others were familiar faces, now of course older, as I myself must have appeared to them. One averted his gaze as if, I thought, to avoid having to acknowledge me. Another, as I passed him by, was evidently surprised, though nothing more, as in the case of the poet Naborí, who looked at me for some time but made no move to greet me as I walked by him toward the back of the patio where I could wait alone for the door of the hall to open.

Up to that moment the atmosphere was frigid. At the back of the patio where I was standing a group of people clustered around the organizer of the function, a high-ranking official of the UNEAC whom I had known since my youth. (I omit his name for reasons of discretion and because it would add nothing to the value of the anecdote.) He expressed surprise at my presence, and he surprised me in turn by suddenly leaving his group and coming over to offer his hand, a smile, and a cordial greeting. We stepped a bit away from the crowd and he asked me in a low voice utterly free of hostility. "You've paid, then, your debt to society?" "Yes," I replied, "completely." "Well," he remarked, "you've settled up and don't owe a thing . . ." He said this as if it were the most natural thing in the world. "No, on the contrary," I responded, "it's me they owe something to; they overcharged." I smiled. There was a pause as if he were taking time to digest my answer. His cordial expression, however, never changed. He immediately shifted topics. He spoke of our youth together, recalling how we met. He was somewhat younger and began to write and publish his first poems when I was already beginning to be established. We also recalled our modest work together in the fight against Batista, and of his present role in Cuban cultural life. After another pause he remarked to me in a confidential tone, "I have followed your situation in recent years. I know all about the propaganda launched on your behalf abroad." Yet another pause, after which he added condescendingly, "Well, if it's all on behalf of a great poet, I guess there's nothing wrong with that. But in the case of others . . ." At that moment, the lecturer arrived and we all started to move into the hall.

The lecture was preceded by some introductory remarks about the visitor, delivered precisely by the man with whom I had been conversing a few moments before. They were entirely non-political, merely a recital of his curriculum vitae. I enjoyed the talk, which was an interesting exposition concerning one of the great poets of the Spanish language. When it was over, as I moved toward the platform, my way was blocked by an old acquaintance, who made a gesture of indifference combined with irritation. Prior to 1959, by reason of a poetic anthology and some

Cuadra reading his poem *Canto de amor al Alma Mater* on the occasion of his law class reunion banquet, 1956.

articles of mine, and others that were written about me as well in the [Havana] newspaper *El Mundo*, he attacked me literarily, and I had responded. He made his attacks from the pages of the newspaper *Tiempo en Cuba*, owned by [Batista ally] Rolando Masferrer. When the case of Heberto Padilla became a *cause célèbre*, he was one of those who fell into disgrace. Evidently he had since found a way of resurfacing on the literary scene. As he tried to block my way, I pushed him aside and continued to the lectern to have a few words with the visitor. I did not look back to register his reaction.

As I was leaving, at the door I once again ran into the old friend I had been speaking to upon my arrival. He greeted me again warmly, and bade me farewell saying, "Don't be a stranger, come back some other day. There are a lot of functions here that'll interest you. Really, I'm very glad to see you." We shook hands. I too had reason to rejoice in our meeting.

IX

The second time I went to a public meeting at the Writers' Union was somewhat later, in my final years on the island. It must have been at the end of 1984 or the beginning of 1985. The motive was a poetry reading which featured a woman writer, one of my oldest and staunchest friends. I went in the same cautious, wary spirit as before, determined to speak only to those who took the first step. It turned out better than before: an occasional person tried to ignore or avoid me, and a few (many more) recognizing me, came up to say hello. There I ran into David Fernández.

I knew David when he was very young, younger, in fact, than I. He was a troubled boy, confused, unstable, in need of love and affection and also in sore need of a sense of identity, self-worth, and direction in life. The son of divorced parents and with a younger sister, from adolescence he was compelled to contribute to the sustenance of the household. His mother was poor, a foreigner of little character; he was devoted to her and she to him. As an adolescent he worked as an actor, not the most abundant or regular source of income. In his search for personal identity he discovered poetry and used it as a shortcut with the same enthusiasm with which he jumped into two or three marriages. (Followed by as many divorces, in which I represented him as his lawyer, as I did in two criminal cases, when he had committed offenses while under the influence of alcohol. On both occasions I was able to win his acquittal.)

I think it likely that members of the old communist party actively courted him even before 1959, because during the first moment of the revolutionary triumph in January we ran into each other one night at the University of Havana. It was odd to see him there, since he was not a student at the time. But in those first days almost nobody knew what to do. That informal meeting was one of many that were held, and to which one went to affirm one's views, above all for those of us who were

graduates of the University. But there were people of all kinds of
backgrounds there.

On that occasion I recall David as very active, vehemently
shouting revolutionary slogans. "What are you doing here?" I
asked him. "Nothing special, just agitating," he responded in a
jovial, euphoric fashion. "Agitating, for what?" He answered, in
a joking tone of voice, "The party sent me." "Party, what party?" I
asked him sarcastically, as if questioning a little boy telling obvious untruths. He winked at me and made a theatrical gesture
which suggested that I didn't need to be told. I paid no attention,
dismissing it all as one of his many capers, and with a cordial pat
on the back I left him to his devices.

With time he began to show a decided loyalty to the Revolution and its works, following every twist and turn of its party
line. At the First Meeting of Writers in 1960 in Camagüey we met
each other once again. Whenever he grabbed the microphone
he showed himself to be the most ardent and shrillest of participants. I believe he was the first Cuban I ever heard sing the
"Internationale." He gave himself over to a life of both literature
and action, now enjoying the support of the powers that be. He
drank. But he was writing too and getting better at it. All those
years, I think he was hard at work in militant journalism and in
the Writers' Union. In poems of his I read from time to time
his revolutionary sentiments were always evident. And really, it
could have been a case of conviction just as well as of necessity. Who knows? I thought. And now here we were, at a special
occasion, meeting again.

I would never have taken the initiative to go over to him were
he not standing with my friend, whose poetry was to be read
that day. It was she who summoned me. The greeting was a bit
cool—certainly cautious—on both sides. He had changed a lot
since I had last seen him twenty years before. Heavier, more serious, grayer at the temples, more measured in his gestures. So,
there we were, the three of us, talking in a cordial fashion. He

knew, of course, my whole story. He managed to touch upon the subject in the most oblique manner possible—that much I'll say. We spoke about him. He was no longer in thrall to alcohol. He was given over almost completely to his writing, and he had a government job in some office the name of which I've forgotten. The nature of his work required the use of the intellect. When I asked him about his family, he told me that his mother and sister had both left the country and that he was living alone. I did not need to express my sympathy, for he anticipated whatever I might have said by assuring me that he felt fully compensated by the life he now led within the Revolution.

I thought about the distant days of his youth, his former life, and I admitted to myself that David had finally found an outlet in his present role. Those of his writings I later read, more or less sporadically, seemed to me to be sincere, and I ended by classifying him in the category of the intellectual who, not merely in his outward aspect or in his work but also in his life, is truly integrated into the political system in which he lives and is at peace with it.

X

A rather different consideration would apply to cases like José A. Baragaño, who died some years ago, at least if what I learned about him is true. I qualify my remarks, because I was not a witness to what I am about to relate, although the person who told me the story is normally a very reliable source.

First, I want to go back in time and recount one antecedent needed to make the fullest and most balanced judgment of the case. In 1957, when the Renuevo literary group was established, its founders (I was one) sponsored a series of meetings to which various writers and poets of our generation were invited. The purpose was to analyze some proposals which our group thought were relevant to our generational tasks, both with respect to literary work and the country's broader needs. The meetings took place in the pleasant home of Ana Rosa Núñez in Marianao, a municipality next to Havana.

There, Baragaño, whom I had never met before, adopted an extremely intemperate posture, well described by Alberto Baeza Flores, who was also present, in his book *Cuba: The Laurel and the Palm*. Baragaño had just returned from Paris waving the banners of surrealism, and his position on everything—social problems, revolutions, general tasks and sacrifices, etc.—was one of total skepticism and disbelief. Of all of those assembled there he was most at odds with the notion of revolution and the social struggle. In fact, he walked out of the meeting in a cloud of anathemas and denunciations.

This will explain why, in the first days of 1959, I was dumbstruck to see him at a meeting of writers and artists at the home of General Bayo, at Tarará Beach, where enthusiasm ran strong for the Revolution in its uncertain, hopeful early course.

Later, when the cultural organisms of the Revolution began to be established, a person whose work I trust told me that Baragaño tried to recruit him for either the Writers' Union or some other body, arguing that it was a good opportunity for artists and writers to "get involved," that all one had to do was to write things in favor of the Revolution, and presto! one would obtain economic support, positions, special privileges—in fine, altogether a small price to pay to be permitted to write on a full-time basis, publish, and so forth.

I know nothing of his subsequent career. He may have experienced a transformation which went beyond appearances, but if the anecdote is true, one must question the sincerity of his revolutionary poems, which were written in a flat, open style utterly at variance with his earlier work.

Cases like this one—I cite it as one example among many—are very different from that of David Fernández. In the first instance, one can perceive a genuine integration into the Revolution and the country's established political system, seeing a man or woman's work as the logical expression of his or her deepest artistic and human commitments. In the second, however, the loyalty to the regime expressed in one's published work is an artful lie.

XI

At the beginning of this essay I stated frankly that in matters of culture and politics one must begin by acknowledging that in Cuba today there exist writers both in favor of and opposed to the existing system. But it is also true that we must go beyond that simple dichotomy, since even among many of those who are part of the official culture and who march in the stage army of revolutionary writers there are many variations and nuances. Sometimes individual circumstances are not easy to analyze or understand. Without question a revolutionary process introduces new themes and aesthetic attitudes into prevailing artistic trends. In the Cuban case there was a total change of direction. In terms of what interests us here, it is of greater moment to observe how the specifically national factors have reacted or evolved, because these after all are what are reflected in artistic production. Those who fundamentally, without any previous record as revolutionaries or communists, now appear as such, are simply reflecting the country's social, human and political environment. I am not, therefore, concerned here with Cuba's old-line Marxists, since for purposes of this analysis there is no reason to question the revolutionary commitment of people like Nicolás Guillén, Juan Marinello, Navarro Luna, and others of later generations who were Marxists well before the Revolution.

But in the case of others one must proceed with a good dose of genuine curiosity and speculative understanding, taking into fullest account the human and transcendental dimensions. Above all, one must avoid utterly black-and-white categories.

To attend cultural events in today's Havana is an interesting experience. In the Old City one of the sites richest in colonial atmosphere is the Plaza de Armas. At night, bounded by the Palace of

the Captains-General, the Templete with its symbolic *ceiba* tree,
the old La Fuerza fortress, and the Palace of the Segundo Cabo, it
all appears as if time had stopped. On one of my last days in Cuba
I read in a newspaper that at the Palace of the Segundo Cabo a
party was being held to celebrate the publication of an anthology
of Cuban poets of the 1950s, that is, my own generation. It was
a curious experience to pick up a copy to see who was included
and who was not. I was already busy with the details of my departure and bidding good-bye to many people. I took advantage
of this event to bid farewell to a writer friend I knew would be
present. It was my last contact with the Cuban cultural world.

Almost all of the rooms of the old Palace—recently recon-
structed—are fitted out for museum exhibitions. Otherwise it
appears as it always did, with its patio enclosed by the walls
and balconies on higher floors, with an ornamental fountain
and plants in the center. A beautiful place which at one time
served as the seat of the nation's Supreme Court. Those in at-
tendance were, naturally, mainly poets and writers. There were
more familiar faces than at the other functions I had previously
attended. I proceeded as prudently as on my two previous visits
to the Writers' Union. Here, as there, some people avoided me,
others took the first step and approached me.

I spoke with the friend I had come to take leave of, after buy-
ing the anthology and discussing it with her. I was just about to
leave when I recognized a poet two or three steps away, gazing
at me with amazement. He continued to stare at me, evidently
troubled by the sight, when another poet who had been speaking with us passed by him. The former caught him by the arm,
and the two had a brief conversation in a low tone of voice. His
question apparently answered, he looked at me again, but this
time with greater amazement. Then he came toward me with
open arms, which wrapped around me in frank embrace. And
with evident emotion he dragged me into the next room, where
there were no people and where we could talk privately. His surprise was even more justified by the coincidence that the day

before: "I was looking through your book of poems once more; what a fine poet you are!" He referred to my first book of verse that I must have given him more than twenty years before. He knew I was out of jail, because some time before, "X . . . told me he had seen you on Twenty-third Street." I asked him if this individual, a writer, knew me personally and was acquainted with my work. "Almost all of us here know all about you, though not everyone is disposed to tell you so."

I learned that he had fallen out of favor some years back, that for quite a time he lived under a cloud. But with time he had managed to work his way back to intellectual respectability and literary relevance. He was once again a star in the firmament of Cuban cultural life.

We had a warm, I should even say affectionate, conversation. We avoided direct political topics and concentrated on matters personal and human. We nonetheless spoke as well about various aspects of the cultural scene, in which we had both been participants or witnesses. In his view future generations would understand things better and adapt more easily. For his part he hoped his children would turn out to be good revolutionaries, so that they would not be at odds with the society in which they were obliged to live.

He asked me if I was thinking of leaving the country. I said yes, though I found it painful to be separated from my homeland, which I loved and for which I had suffered. He assented to this statement with considerable empathy; he was as respectful of my person and my circumstances as if they were his own. He also expressed his love for Cuba, and above all for Havana, which for him was a place without equal. And finally, as if summoning up his deepest thoughts, he said to me tenderly, "I can never leave. This is where Plácido and Zenea and Martí died, you see? I want to live in my own country, die in my own country, and be part of its national literature." He wished me much luck, and with another embrace we parted.

I made no effort to mull over any of these things; I put them into my heart, the only place capable of treating them with a deeper understanding, such as renders every individual an entity wholly unto himself, and for that reason, in perpetual isolation.

I walked out of the old colonial palace and stood for a moment looking at the Plaza de Armas. Then I went down one of the streets of the old quarter, carrying with me this last experience that—in a fashion—squared the circle, that is, answered the questions which occurred to me on my first days out of prison, returning to my native city. "Where are the poets, the writers, the artists? What are they doing? How do they stand with respect to their circumstances?"

As I neared the port, weaving my way through ancient facades, Havana appeared to me—painful to say—more beautiful than ever, as all things must appear when we are forced to part with them. And I sensed as never before the soul of the city, a soul unique in time, the common patrimony of all of us who have discovered it and who continue to cherish it.

The End (1985)

A Postscript

It is now over seven years that I left Cuba. Havana, my town, lies out there, distant yet near in mind and heart. It is also part of my here and now because of the news I get from the Island: letters, reports, books, and the testimony of arriving Cubans.

Much has changed in the circumstances and activities of writers and artists in recent years. In June 1991 a public letter signed by ten Cuban writers and intellectuals became an international news item. These writers demanded that the government take into account the nation's intellectuals in the solution of national problems which constitute an undisguisable crisis; and they demanded political and economic changes in the country; an unusual event in the cultural and political history of these three decades of revolution and totalitarianism. Something that was inconceivable a few years back, particularly when some of the signatories were active members of the National Union of Cuban Writers and Artists.

What has taken place during these seven years in the Cuban cultural field? A brief synthesis of the facts will complete by and large my vision of "Writers in Socialist Cuba" which I carried to exile in 1985.

In what we term the "official culture"—the one that the state promotes and which is the only one that is recognized and published by the media—an ample artistic-literary production is being maintained which the publishing houses disseminate in extensive editions. They are works, of course, that hew to the line that Fidel Castro marked in 1961: With the Revolution, everything; against the Revolution, nothing.

But for over two years now a new phenomenon has been taking place. Some writers and a few artists have adopted a public attitude of confrontation or dissidence with regard to official aesthetic policy and political doctrine. The fact has coincided with the appearance in Cuba of groups in favor of human rights, peaceful resistance, or civil disobedience who demand of the government respect for the tenets of the Universal Declaration of Human Rights originally proclaimed by the United Nations Organization.

The new outbreak of dissident art and literature met a corresponding reciprocity in the human rights groups. And several of these writer and artist dissidents joined the ranks of the activist groupings in a shift from nonconforming literature and art to open political confrontation. It led a few painters to organize independent groups, like those calling themselves "The Association for a Free Art" (APAL), "Street Art," and "Art and Freedom," which put on exhibits in private homes and in the streets, all of them repressed by the police and popular attack groups under government encouragement and organization. Among these painters we shall remark two: Juan Enrique González, currently in exile, and Jorge Crespo Díaz, sentenced to prison in Cuba.

The most outstanding cases among the writers are Roberto Luque Escalona and María Elena Cruz Varela. The former wrote in Cuba and published abroad an essay titled "Fidel: el juicio de la historia" ("The Tiger's Sons" in English). After many vicissitudes Luque Escalona recently went into exile.

María Elena Cruz Varela was the winner of the national poetry prize Julián del Casal in 1989. In 1990 she addressed to Castro himself an open public letter of inconformity with the government's policies. She signed on to the already cited letter of the ten intellectuals in 1991. Not long afterwards, hordes of street gangs organized by the government under the banner of "Rapid Response Brigades" assaulted María Elena's home. She was beaten, dragged to the street and forced to eat flyers issued by a pacifist and human rights group known as "Criterio alternativo," of which she was one of the founders. After this aggression María Elena was subjected to a summary political trial in which she was condemned to two years' loss of liberty.

A number of writers and artists have felt the necessity of expressing themselves in a completely independent way in art and literature. As an example, in the city of Matanzas a rustic, handsome art and literature review has continually been published under the title of La Revista del Vigía. It is not edited by any official entity, nor is it printed by a state-owned press. It is a handmade magazine, a labor of craftsmanship. Three editions are published yearly. Each edition consists of two hundred copies, done in brown paper, bound one by one. Its articles, stories, and poems are either handwritten or typed; and its drawings and cartoons are done with fountain pen, pencil, or ballpoint pen. But the result of this nearly primitive work is that of an exquisite product, doubtlessly done with greater artistic and literary quality and, of course, with greater originality than the publications of the official organs in which several of its same editors work. La Revista del Vigía is put together in their free time and outside their official workplace.

This publication is not a question of dissident literature; it has no direct or indirect political content or projection; nor is it a literature of official slogans or of opposition, not even a literature of escape. La Revista del Vigía is something else in the midst of the Cuban cultural context; it does not take sides; rather it occupies a higher, possibly timeless level, like a brief oasis in the national culture.

At the background of the scenario heretofore described, Cuban cultural life projects itself as a changing world where each new day may spring a surprise. Every day, in my far-off exile, I get news; and I recompose the image of the political and cultural life of the country that I brought with me seven years ago. So often do writers, artists, and intellectuals flee the Island, deserting its political regime, while other writers' and artists' names break into official publications within the Island for the first time. And some make their way into the dissident ranks.

Not long ago I watched on television a daring film report on Havana. I saw the familiar streets of my aged city, the crumbling facades, the empty buildings, as well as some things that were unknown to me. Upon this stage, I reflected, this changing world that I have described continues to develop, modifying and completing the vision and testimony I brought out in 1985 . . . . One thing remains the same: Havana's seaside drive, the Malecón, sea wall and sea at odds. And the eternal Cuban, here sitting, there walking, by the sea, across from the centuries-old Castle that keeps guarding the bay . . . and ever the sea. . . .

Miami, 1992

A Correspondence of Poems (from Jail)

Angel Cuadra
Translated by Donald D. Walsh

Cuba, May 1979

Dear Juana Rosa:

I don't know the date when this letter will reach you. Maybe it won't reach you, like so many others that haven't had the "loving mailman" that you yearn for in your poem. Now that "mailman" does indeed exist—on this one occasion—and he has all my affection and confidence. I shall also try to get some poems to you (you see: "the height of letters").

Don't be surprised that I use, as if they were mine, terms and expressions of yours. When you read my poems to yourself you'll understand (as you already know) this identification with you, with your verses, with your world that I've entered as though it were my own.

I've written you two letters before this one in the past month. I'm afraid you didn't get them. And they're almost impossible to duplicate, for you'll notice that I'm writing you with no carbon copy.

The first of the two preceding letters is the answer to your letter of March 11, after two years without news of you. But the second (which must have been sent to your aunt's house and which is the one that interests me most) has essential things, questions, answers, affirmations, openings into what is possible and essential. Its existence is the result of having rescued—after

two years in the hands of someone else—three letters of yours
two years before, March 3, 8, and 29 of 1977 and thirteen poems
of Sea and Letters and Hours. For me everything is of tremen-
dous importance. Marvelous poems, with a flight even greater
than the initial ones that I received in 1976 (and they stripped
me as a consequence of my new unjust imprisonment: the crime
of lèse-poetry). I explained to you in this letter that I had read
your poems before almost a choir of initiates, my comrades here,
poets and lovers of poetry, to whom my voice transmitted—
they sitting on the floor—your message of cosmic and general
love, as if you were visiting us and you were for each one of us
"tender keeper of the keys" surviving "in a ray of light towards
the others." There were guitars and songs. One of the musicians
and poets, fascinated by "Night of Bread," promised to set it to
music. And this morning, guitar in hand, he brought me your
poem with music in which you now spread toward the ambit of
the musical staff.

I then understood what you had already grasped before, how
original and transcendental were the themes of Sea in the poetry
of the continent and in the possibilities of our culture. The importance, besides, of its marriage with Impromptus. And something more that presented itself to me as a mission and as a kind
of challenge: my response to your Sea in harmonic and symbolic
correspondence. It was—it still is—heartbreaking and heartening, this tacit assignment. Not if your letters and poems had arrived two years before. But now I have only days: the challenge
accepted—a living mission, the heartening heartbreak of having
to write a poem a day, without polishing, without resting one
night, without taking time. The task is perhaps the hardest that
has ever faced any poet. For I can't choose the free theme; in
order to achieve the correspondence and unity that I hope for
between your poems and my hasty ones, I have to write under
coercion, like a native troubadour; I must insert myself between
one verse and the next in your poems (and letters) that I reread
every day. Respond poem to poem, refashion your phrases. Bring

forth each poem of mine from one of yours, as if it were bred in it like cause and effect, in what you call "our relationship." I want your opinion.

Our mailman—my friend—will talk to you at greater length. My poems reach you freshly written, almost as though I had just talked with you . . . and how I wish I could talk to you as long as that long and beautiful duty that you asked for, "kindling the dreams."

I have no idea of what my immediate future will be. I tell you only that there has been no legal basis for this new reprisal against me. Only that I am a poet. That the world speaks of me, that you, for example, transcend me through your verses; that I do not deny my song, nor do I make it kneel down, nor do I use it for other ends either political or partisan but only literary, universal, timeless.

It is important for you to emphasize this.

Now while night passes and the bars forbid me even a little light from outside, I think that I have come to visit you in your "house of transparency."

A hug and love from

Angel

Postscript (June)

You'll be surprised by this June postscript. The first route didn't work. But life granted that another friend (who will have to be nameless) will be the epistolary bridge for us by a more fitting route. The mailman will now carry to your house, after a long and distant journey, all my poems for you. They are the answers to your books that I spoke to you about, but now finished, as another book of poems. We'll call it A *Correspondence of Poems* (from Jail), this parenthesis as a complementary subtitle below.

You'll see that they were written between 29 April and 5 June, quite a marathon. As I said to you in the first letter, they come forth as though from your poems (which was to be expected from us in our unheard-of relationship), and therefore almost all of them have epigraphs from your poems or your letters. (It occurs to me that the references are sufficient, although it might be better to locate each epigraph in your complete poem separately, in smaller type, but this is complicated.) In short, the marvelous challenge of your poems, accepted by me as a mission, that one that you call "irreversible luminous cycle" or in the "Irresistible affinities" that you quote, or Teilhard's phrase "the fullness of the cosmic function of love," which in us is Poetry. Have I, have we, been able to fulfill the plan? If we take it on as the unusual and therefore as "quite natural" as you point out, it is possible, I don't believe there is any other similar occurrence in Spanish-American poetry. I have not had (nor did I want) time for revision: you receive them in their state of nature, newborn; children born to us both.

If you read them in the order in which I have arranged them you'll get the atmosphere more exactly.

(from Cuba, July 12, 1979)
[final fragment of the letter]

You see that I write with no order, even with some fear, for it is risky in this place. But to hell with fears, for they'll never confine me if it's a question of doing greater things.

Maybe in a few days I'll be out of jail. Perhaps, as the final poem says, the "sea behind bars" can be left behind (the root, I mean, not the fruit).

A hug, and a hope that we can soon summon up these things in a visit at the window you mention.

Angel

Ritual of Water

For I know you only through your writings,
of all my friends,
you are the least unknown.

Juana Rosa

You speak my name—
your paper lips,
your breath of distance—
and in your ghostly accent you touch my ear from within
as if you were naming me from an inner plane,
calling outside.

I identify myself now
in baptismal wonder.

Ritual of water.
You place yourself at the center of the myth.
At what scale of time was the appointment?
In what world of yesterday was this dialogue left hanging?
This familiar bread that you offer me
was it perhaps from another alliance of my hunger and
    your wheat?

Your dew-covered hand comes
and puts my name on my forehead from within.
You call to me and I follow you
through those "labyrinths of the infinite" that you display
from your baptismal lips.

April 29

Ritual del Agua

Pues sólo te conozco por lo escrito
eres de mis amigos
el menos extranjero.

                                        Juana Rosa

Dices mi nombre
—tus labios de papel,
tu aliento de distancia—,
y en tu acento fantasma tocas mi oído por dentro
como si me nombraras desde un plano interior,
llamando afuera.

Me identifico ahora
en bautismal asombro.

Ritual del agua.
Te sitúas en el centro del mito.
¿En qué escala del tiempo fue la cita?
¿En qué mundo de ayer quedó pendiente este diálogo?
Este pan conocido que me ofreces
¿fue acaso de otra alianza de mi hambre y tu trigo?

Viene tu mano de relente
y me pone mi nombre en la frente por dentro.
Me llamas y te sigo
por esos "laberintos de infinito" que estrenas
desde tus labios de bautismo.

                                        Abril 29

The Task

> like one who can
> display against the light
> a chaliced territory.
>   Juana Rosa

My dear,
when you go about the world
with overcoat and hair,
with the exact brand of skin
and abstract papers that keep falling from your hands;
when you drop my name in the carelessness of a gesture,
and have to give explanations—
because they always ask for them—
concerning a mystery so simple
that it has no need for alphabets;
and they ask you about my face, which you don't know,
and about my character which you have known since birth,
because you bore it
in a birth of bread and tears . . .
don't utter, of the shadows of my iron bars, more than
    the sign,
don't speak of the vultures that scratch at me
for crumbs of hatred
and take light from the human clay;
speak to them of the poem that I defend
against a corrosion not from my iron bars,
tell them about the strophe-symbol in which I am
the link of a transparent fire
on the move from the depths of time;
of the leaf beneath the north wind that persists
in the timeless verdure;
of the clear duty
to cultivate "a chaliced territory"

for the possible display against the light
and confess to them that is why
you have wished to save the verse of which I am composed.

May 1

Encargo

> como quien puede
> estrenar a contraluz
> un territorio cáliz.
> Juana Rosa

Amiga,
cuando vayas por el mundo
con abrigo y cabellos,
con la precisa marca de piel
y papeles abstractos que se te van cayendo de las manos;
cuando dejes rodar mi nombre en el descuido de un gesto,
y tengas que dar explicaciones
—porque siempre las piden—
al asunto de un misterio tan simple
que le sobran alfabetos;
y te pregunten por mi rostro que no sabes
y por la índole que tú sí me conoces desde el parto,
porque la diste al mundo
en un alumbramiento de pan y lágrimas . . .
no digas, de las sombras de mis rejas, más que el signo;
no digas de los buitres que me escarban
por migajas de odio,
y quitan luz al barro humano;
háblales del poema que defiendo
contra un óxido que no es el de las rejas;
diles de la estrofa-símbolo en que soy
el eslabón de un fuego transparente

que marcha desde el fondo de los tiempos;
de la hoja bajo el cierzo que persiste
en el verdor intemporal;
del claro oficio
de cultivar "un territorio cáliz"
para el estreno a contraluz posible . . .
y confiésales que, por eso,
tú has querido salvar el verso en que consisto.

Mayo 1

Colloquy of Sadness

Through your prison cell you go, I through my song.
                                           Juana Rosa

At times I start to look outside
and I take my bones out of these four walls.
It has rained too much sand
and one wants to prove to himself that he's alive,
for there are chains and chains . . . and you're helpless
with so many shackles.
But foam flows, one thinks,
and it seems that God is smiling . . . Well, it's just a phrase.

Because I take myself out of here
as if I were pulling myself by the hair,
like a drop overflowing the glass
and falling outside.
And I seek your warm friendship
that comes to me in reflections.
You who have no face.
And we set out walking like old
travelling companions
who usually say things that others don't understand
or aren't interested in
or it's like a silly remark in the eye of reason,
that leaves dialectics squinting.

And yet, for you,
"it's so fantastic that it seems to you quite natural."
And I add "and so good."
But it seems that I stumble on a stone
because I get up off the ground . . .
I mean: I return. And I am struck by

Vallejo's verse:
"how long are these walls four."
It is then that I notice that you are a bit of poem
brought by the wind,
and I an anchor buried in the desert
and that, in truth, like strangers
"through my cell I go, you through your song."

May 3

Coloquial de lo Triste

Tú por tu celda vas, yo por mi canto.
Juana Rosa

A veces me pongo a mirar hacia afuera
y me saco los huesos de estas 4 paredes.
Ha llovido demasiada arena
y uno quiere afirmarse que está vivo,
porque hay cadenas y cadenas . . . y no se puede más
con tanto grillo.
Pero afluyen espumas; se piensa,
y parece que Dios sonríe . . . Bueno, es un decir.

Porque me saco de aquí
como tirándome del pelo
como una gota que el vaso desborda
y cae fuera.
Y busco tu amistad tibia
que me viene de reflejos.
Tú que no tienes rostro.
Y nos ponemos a andar como antiguos
compañeros de viaje
que suelen hablar de lo que los demás no entienden

o no les interesa
o es como un disparate en el ojo del juicio,
que deja bizca a la dialéctica.

Y para ti, no obstante,
"es tan fantástico que te parece lo más natural."
Y yo agrego . . . "y tan bueno".
Pero parece que tropiezo con una piedra,
porque me levanto del suelo . . .
quiero decir: regreso. Y me golpea
el verso de Vallejo:
"hasta dónde son 4 estas paredes".
Es entonces que advierto que tú eres un pedazo de poema
por el viento traído,
y yo un ancla clavada en el desierto
y que, en verdad extranjeros,
"yo por mi celda voy, tú por tu canto".

                                          Mayo 3

The Day Your Letter Comes

You won't receive this letter
because it has no wings
to outwit walls.

                    Juana Rosa

The days are so fierce
there's no difference between them
and there have been so many years of these twin days
that the day your letter comes
is an almanac event.
That day a name is born to time;
so much so that they've ended up being classified:
nameless days
and the day your letter comes.

Your letter is the poem brought by the dawn.

It seemed as though today was the day:
there were heralds and signals,
a sunless shine climbed up the walls,
there was wounded music in the barbed wire.

And it must have been then that
they broke your letter's wings
like a carrier pigeon: the falcons
intercepted it.

Inside the envelope
the word smothered,
like a criminal abortion to beauty
engendered for nobody.

Night falls like a curtain;
everything goes back to being as it was.

In front of my cell
nameless, endless days
go by.

May 2

El Día de Tu Carta

> Esta carta que no recibirás
> porque no tiene alas
> para burlar los muros.
> Juana Rosa

Son tan fieros los días
que no se diferencian
y han sido tantos años de estos días gemelos,
que el día de tu carta
es un acontecimiento de almanaques.
Ese día le nace nombre al tiempo;
tanto, que han terminado por clasificarse:
días sin nombre
y el día de tu carta.

Tu carta es el poema que trae el alba.

Hoy parecía que era:
había heraldos y señales,
trepó un brillo sin sol sobre los muros,
había música herida en los alambres.

Y debió ser entonces cuando
le quebraron las alas a tu carta
como paloma de mensaje: la interceptaron
gerifaltes.

Dentro del sobre
se asfixió la palabra,

como crimen de aborto a la belleza
engendrada para nadie.

Cae la noche como un trapo;
todo vuelve a ser como antes.
Frente a mi celda
días sin nombre, interminables,
pasan de largo.

Mayo 2

Your Poems That I Never Got

I'm afraid you're not getting my letters . . .
a very short letter handwritten and
accompanied by four poems.

Juana Rosa

Your poems that I never got,
that undertook their journey across the dew
and ended up in captivity and shipwreck;
your naked words
sent
in a first edition
by your hand
for my hands and my eyes;
devoured by wolves in their travel
through a wood,
messengers of a soulful food
confiscated in bites;
their echoes must be,
like ghosts of sound,
dragged from the wind
by dark trees,
cold sands and roads
because, in the night,
when the breeze plays on the walls and the bars,
it brings a kind of presence of harmonies
that's not precisely music.

May 23

Tus Poemas Que Nunca Recibí

Temo que no estés recibiendo mis cartas . . .
una carta muy corta escrita a mano y
acompañada por cuatro poemas.
                                        Juana Rosa

Tus poemas que nunca recibí,
que emprendieron su viaje a través del rocío
y dieron en capturas y naufragios;
tus palabras desnudas,
enviadas
en primera edición
de tu mano
para mis manos y mis ojos;
devorados por lobos en su marcha
por un bosque,
mensajeros de un alimento de alma
a dentelladas confiscado;
deben de estar sus ecos,
como fantasmas de sonido,
arrastrados del viento
por árboles oscuros,
frías arenas y caminos,
porque, en las noches,
cuando la brisa ronda sobre los muros y las rejas,
trae como una presencia de armonías
que no es precisamente música.
                                        Mayo 23

Police Efficiency

Poetry is the height of letters.
Juana Rosa

Your poems have got lost.
I wasn't in the house.
But they came in with arms, with orders,
with many evil intentions,
prying into corners.
A gust of terror
scattered papers across the floor.
They went looking for crimes preserved in envelopes;
words that let their echoes trail
like the gossamer of the stars.
They found crimes like these:
"the first year of the dream,
we are poets; therefore we love,
as a child I remember a courtyard,
of my elbows in the rainbow,
the violet ash,
or April that stood on tiptoe to brush your angel . . ."
And they finally came upon the accomplished crime
under your name of distance,
a perfect epistolary crime:
your poems,
"the height of letters."

                                                        May 4

Eficacia Policial

La poesía es el colmo de las cartas.
Juana Rosa

Se han perdido tus poemas.
Yo no estaba en la casa.
Pero entraron con armas, con órdenes,
con muchas ganas de mal,
husmeando los rincones.
Una ráfaga de terror
dispersó los papeles por el piso.
Iban buscando crímenes conservados en sobres;
palabras que descolgaban sus ecos
como los flecos de las estrellas.
Encontraron delitos como estos:
"el primer año del sueño,
somos poetas, luego, amamos,
recuerdo un patio de mi infancia,
de codos en el arcoiris,
la ceniza morada,
o abril que se empinaba hasta rozarte el ángel . . ."
Y al fin dieron con el delito consumado
bajo tu nombre de distancia,
crimen epistolar perfecto:
tus poemas,
"el colmo de las cartas".

Mayo 4

Answer to Your "Letter to My Island"

Island,
far from you is near the most
sensitive point
of time's wound:
far from you is absolute solitude.
                                    Juana Rosa

My dear,
you have lent me your eyes inside an envelope
to look at the island from your distance.

I answer you also with eyes on loan
that reflect the other face
of the island that we love and that grieves us—
our face, I explain—
the one that complements the solitude you mention
with the other solitude.

Island,
more than as a land of substance,
I have the right to love you beyond
judicial verdicts,
beyond the new names with which
they baptize the ancient places.
You are also my neighborhood corner,
my feet book laden on the staircase,
the love that I knew,
the poem that I said one open night in Havana
with friends and dreams,
the blood I shared
and the fear and the hope,
the enthusiasm that is shared
and the enthusiasm divided up because
it's not the heritage of anyone.

You are the sea that surrounds you
and the ship.
You are the faces of those who hate me
and the faces of those who love me.
And, since a friend with distant music
names me
and ransoms me in the "symbolic eye"
in which you burn,
you are also "the tender scrawl
of an absent writer"
on transparent blackboards.
Of this you also consist,
and you rise up.

When I came back to your streets—
scarcely a few hours . . . or perhaps centuries of urgency—
gray-haired and scarred by bars,
I went to look for you in the wells of memory,
where you no longer were,
I looked for you in familiar corners,
I lifted the stones of my streets
without finding a trace of you.
And in the tree where you no longer were,
in the old neighbor who left a tear in my arms,
in the confusion of names,
in the strange hymns . . .
I felt my glance a stranger.
I thought of the story of Zhivago
returning to his old city
and on his face "all the windows of the world
half-closed toward the void."
I broke the mirror that was casting its image at me
in an oracular litany.
And I went up the street through the night
in pieces,

in pieces the shadow within,
in pieces the rage,
and the anguish in pieces.
And in pieces an inexpressive tenderness
that from my solitude went mounting
up to the solitude of the stars.

My dear,
I complement the solitude you mention,
with this other
solitude of uprooting.

   P.S.
Tonight
at the edge of the iron bars, I confess to you:
in time's wound where the island grieves
there was, under a cosmic miracle,
an irrational urge
to go on loving her.

                                      May 6

Respuesta a tu "Carta a mi isla"

> Isla,
> lejos de ti es cerca del punto
> más sensible
> de la herida del tiempo:
> lejos de ti es la soledad concreta.
> > Juana Rosa

Amiga,
me has prestado tus pupilas dentro de un sobre,
para mirar la isla desde tu distancia.

Te respondo también con pupilas de préstamo
que reflejan la otra cara
de la isla que amamos y nos duele
—la cara nuestra, aclaro—
la que completa la soledad que dices
con la otra soledad.

Isla,
más que de tierra de substancia,
tengo el derecho de quererte más allá
de los fallos judiciales,
de los nombres nuevos con que
se bautizan los antiguos lugares.
Eres también el rincón de mi barrio,
mis pies con libros por la escalinata,
el amor que conocí,
el poema que dije en una noche abierta de la Habana
con amigos y sueños,
la sangre que compartí
y el miedo y la esperanza;
el entusiasmo que se comparte
y el entusiasmo dividido porque
no es el patrimonio de nadie.
Eres el mar que te rodea
y el barco.
Eres el rostro de los que me odian
y el rostro de los que me aman.
Y, puesto que una amiga de música distante
me nombra,
y me rescata en el "ojo simbólico"
en que ardes,
eres también "el garabato tierno
de un escritor ausente"
sobre pizarras de transparencia.

En esto también consistes,
y te alzas.

Cuando volví a tus calles
—unas horas apenas . . . o quizás siglos de premura—
con cicatrices de rejas y con canas,
fui a buscarte en los pozos del recuerdo,
en donde ya no estabas.
Te busqué por rincones sabidos,
alcé las piedras de mis calles,
sin encontrarte el rastro.
Y en el árbol que ya no estabas,
en la vecina vieja que me dejó una lágrima en los brazos,
en la confusión de los nombres,
en los himnos extraños . . .
sentí extranjera mi mirada.
Pensé en la historia de Zhivago
volviendo a su ciudad antigua
y en su rostro "todas las ventanas del mundo
entornadas hacia la nada".
Rompí el espejo que me lanzaba su imagen
en una letanía de oráculo.
Y seguí calle arriba por la noche,
a pedazos,
a pedazos la sombra dentro,
a pedazos la rabia,
y la angustia a pedazos.
Y a pedazos una ternura indefinible
que desde mi soledad iba subiendo
hasta la soledad de los astros.

Amiga,
te completo la soledad que dices,
con esta otra
soledad del desarraigo.

P.D.
Esta noche,
al borde de las rejas, te confieso:
en la herida del tiempo donde duele la isla
había, bajo un cósmico milagro,
una motivación irrazonable
para seguirla amando.

Mayo 6

Acknowledgment of Receipt

... and like everyone I shall die
of fatal indifference at some moment.

Unless my being loses all restraint
and is displaced
                    by way of love
like a ray of light toward the others.
                                    Juana Rosa

When the night spreads outward
and the hours are dampened by the field,
you don't know how one "dies from existence,"
counting his heartbeats drop by drop.
Along where nothing comes,
much less does love pass
in its sacred servant.
One has learned to die in the daily bread
and from so much yesterday the white hair grows inside.
One can say:
I do not love, therefore I am not;
or I love with no assets,
which is all the indifference of the universe.

Your poem comes
like a stone from the sky
on the still water:
you have splashed my dream
with a "ray of light from the others."

                                          May 15

Acuse de Recibo

. . . y como todos moriré
de fatal desamor algún momento.

A menos que mi ser se desmesure
y sea desplazado
                        vía amor
como rayo de luz hacia los otros.
                                    Juana Rosa

Cuando la noche se extiende afuera
y se mojan las horas por el campo
tú no sabes cómo uno "se muere de existencia",
contando sus latidos gota a gota.
Por donde nada viene,
mucho menos cruza el amor
en su siervo sagrado.
Se ha aprendido a morir en el pan diario
y ya de tanto ayer van las canas por dentro.
Puede decirse:
no amo, luego no soy;
o amo sin posibles,
que es todo el desamor del universo.

Viene el poema tuyo
como piedra de cielo
sobre la inmóvil agua:
me has salpicado el sueño
con un "rayo de luz desde los otros".
                                    Mayo 15

Nameless Ones

> This word
> that jumps from my pen . . .
> love it;
> let yourself fall with eyes shut
> inside it
> as if you did not exist . . .
> for it has no time here.
> Juana Rosa

The word is not yours,
you did not begin its syllables.
You have only
the measure of its music between your lips
now;
not even your voice, for other voices live in it.
In your breath
you bring it from yourself unto my ear:
your hand offers it like "memorable bread"
to my hand.

To hear your word
I have come out of myself—
without my name—
toward a time
that is ours . . . but it spins within another.
I close my eyes and I caress a distant music
in silence.

That word,
like an assignment placed upon your shoulder,
you'll not get to pronounce it
as completely yours,
it will slip on your turn

like a little star;
it will bear our names a minute
"because it has no time here"
where we are only
a verse of the Poem.

                                        May 13–14

Innominados

> Esta palabra
> que salta de mi pluma . . .
> quiérela:
> déjate caer con los ojos cerrados
> dentro de ella
> como si tú no fueras . . .
> porque no tiene tiempo aquí.
>   *Juana Rosa*

No es tuya la palabra,
no iniciaste sus sílabas.
Tienes sólo
el paso de su música entre tus labios
ahora;
ni siquiera tu voz, porque la habitan otras voces.
En tu aliento
la traes desde ti hasta mi oído:
tu mano la ofrece como "pan memorable"
a mi mano.

Para oírtela
he salido de mí
—sin mi nombre—
hacia un tiempo
que es nuestro . . . pero gira dentro de otro.

Cierro los ojos y acaricio una música lejana
en el silencio.

Esa palabra,
como un encargo puesto en tus hombros,
no acabarás de pronunciarla
como completamente tuya;
resbalará sobre tu turno
como un astro pequeño;
llevará nuestros nombres un minuto,
"porque no tiene tiempo aquí"
en donde sólo somos
un verso del Poema.

                                        Mayo 13–14

Vision of the Keys

I glimpse only
a skate rusted by tears
and a very black fountain with some keys
shining up from the bottom.

Juana Rosa

I knew the fountain of the courtyard of your house:
green leaves would fall to the bottom
and a piece of sky would come down like the calm.
I, a visitor,
welcomed by hands
that took care of you as a child.

You were only the name,
the notice on the envelope,
absence.

I wasn't aware of the echo that remains:
your footsteps around the fountain,
your hands at the piano,
the mark of your life in the story,
the space of your body peopled by fish,
the germ of the poem that was going to be,
the keys in the water, eyeless.

Vertigo came to your life:
a spiral of poems and oracles.
And on one of those roads
our letters met
as if we had met one day
in the courtyard of your house.

Today there is prison and distance,
the bridge of the poem

Juana Rosa as a child.

and a mailman of foam.
Time marches forward.

My dear,
magnetized by the dream, we shall go
to the edge of the fountain
and, among toys and Sundays, we shall take the keys
that, at the bottom,
have been waiting for centuries.

                                        May 7–8

Visión de las Llaves

Sólo distingo
un patín oxidado por las lágrimas
y una fuente muy negra donde brillan
desde el fondo unas llaves.

Juana Rosa

Yo conocí la fuente del patio de tu casa:
hojas verdes caían hasta el fondo
y un pedazo de cielo bajaba como calma.
Yo, visitante,
acogido por manos
que te cuidaron en la infancia.

Tú eras el nombre sólo,
la noticia en el sobre,
ausencia.

Yo no advertía el eco que se queda:
tus pasos por la fuente,
tus manos en el piano,
la marca de tu vida en el cuento,
el espacio de tu cuerpo poblado por los peces,
el germen del poema que iba a ser,
las llaves en el agua sin ninguna pupila.

Vino a tu vida el vértigo:
espiral de poemas y oráculos.
Y en un camino de esos
se encontraron nuestras cartas,
como nos hubiésemos encontrado un día
en el patio de tu casa.

Hoy hay la cárcel y la distancia,
el puente del poema

y un cartero de espumas.
El tiempo marcha hacia adelante.

Amiga,
imantados del sueño iremos
al borde de la fuente
y, entre juguetes y domingos, tomaremos las llaves
que, en el fondo,
aguardan hace siglos.

Mayo 7–8

For Your "Night of Bread"

So that night may reach into your cell,
loving, consecrating keeper of the keys.

The ritual illumines the whole world.

    Approach the table
and eat of my body for love
and drink of my blood.

                    Juana Rosa

I have placed myself at the point
at which I let my being drift.
I can't go ahead if I don't assume ecstasy,
if I don't welcome words with other meanings
and go placing them like suns
that begin worlds.
I slither in superior labyrinths, entering
"an irreversible luminous cycle,"
with magic-trail Ariadnes
that I pursue.
I rediscover words,
"vertigo," like the entrance to a spiral of
infinite music;
"ritual," night conducted to my cell
in a loving consecration;
"myth," the solitude denied
by the "memorable bread," become body on my table
and the wine of the blood of the dream.

"Tender keeper of the keys,"
you have brought me night, in a gesture of unction,
into my cell.
In tune with the rite,
I hear your priestly steps arrive;
veils float above the ceremony of your body.

With a canticle of love on your lips
you officiate:
you raise your breast like a chalice
you offer like a naked loaf of bread
your body as food,
your blood as wine . . .

The whole universe is in my cell.

                                        May 9

Por Tu "Noche de Pan"

> para que entre la noche hasta tu celda:
> amorosa llavera consagrando
>
> El rito alumbra todo el universo.
>
>   Acércate a la mesa
> y come de mi cuerpo por amor
> y bebe de mi sangre.
>   Juana Rosa

Me he situado en el punto
en que dejo mi ser a la deriva.
No podría seguir adelante si no asumo el éxtasis,
si no acojo palabras con otros sentidos
y las voy colocando como soles
que inician mundos.
Resbalo en laberintos superiores, entrando
a "un ciclo luminoso irreversible",
con Ariadnas de mágicos rastros
que persigo.
Redescubro los vocablos:
"vértigo", como el ingreso a una espiral de música
infinita;
"rito", la noche conducida hasta mi celda

en una consagración amorosa;
"mito", la soledad negada
por el "pan memorable" hecho cuerpo en mi mesa
y el vino de la sangre del sueño.

"Amorosa llavera",
me has traído la noche, en un gesto de unción,
hasta la celda.
En sinfonía con el rito,
siento llegar tus pasos sacerdotales;
flotan los velos sobre la ceremonia de tu cuerpo.
Con un cántico de amor en los labios
oficias:
alzas como cáliz tu seno:
ofreces como un pan desnudo
tu cuerpo de alimento,
tu sangre como vino . . .

El universo todo está en mi celda.

Mayo 9

Pact

> I've tumbled down the walls of my house
> and now it has transparent curtains . . .
>
> You came to visit me . . .
>
> I beg you to stay forever
> kindling the dreams.
>
> Juana Rosa

A house of transparencies is your house
because you knocked down the walls with tears,
and now its pure shapes consist
of walls of illusion, light, and gauze.

From other sad walls where my life
passes along dark zodiacs,
rescued from evil by your incantations,
I arrive at your door with my scanty star.

Friend of this pact written
in a verse that is missing from the infinite,
of a poem of which we are not the masters.

I have come in answer to your plea to stay
and, in a soul scheme, to reaffirm myself
your accomplice in kindling the dreams.

April 30

Pacto

He tumbado los muros de mi casa
y ahora tiene cortinas transparentes

Viniste a visitarme . . .

te pido que te quedes hasta siempre
atizando los sueños.

Juana Rosa

Casa de transparencias es tu casa
porque tumbaste a lágrimas los muros,
y ahora consisten sus contornos puros
en paredes de ensueño, luz y gasa.

Desde otros muros tristes donde pasa
mi vida por zodíacos oscuros,
rescatado del mal por tus conjuros,
llego a tu puerta con mi estrella escasa.

Amiga de este pacto que está escrito
en un verso que falta al infinito,
de un poema del que no somos dueños,

he acudido a tu ruego de quedarme
y, en un proyecto de almas, reafirmarme
cómplice tuyo en atizar los sueños.

Abril 30

Your Challenge

> . . . I challenge
> anyone who tries to doubt our meeting
> from this Christmas in the sonnet.
>> *Juana Rosa*

Your challenge is the firmness of intent
that, from the hollow of my dark cell,
makes me join in a struggle of beauty,
from death almost to motion.

You affirm, and so you feed
the soul. Your promise of happiness,
like the word of some god, manages to
restore a space and a moment.

The certainty of this meeting is such
that, like a resurrecting Lazarus,
I live on the foretaste of his story.

And, as if returning from another plane,
even without the touch of your hand,
I already have your hand in memory.
>> *May 11–14*

Tu Reto

> . . . Reto
> al que intente dudar de nuestra cita
> desde esta Navidad en el soneto.
>> *Juana Rosa*

Tu reto es la firmeza del intento
que, desde el hueco de mi celda oscura,

me incorpora a una lucha de hermosura,
desde la muerte casi al movimiento.

Afirmas, luego das el alimento
al alma. Tu promesa de ventura,
como palabra de algún dios, procura
instaurar un espacio y un momento.

Es tal la certidumbre de esta cita
que, como Lázaro que resucita,
vivo del anticipo de su historia.

Y, como regresando de otro plano,
aún sin el contacto de tu mano
traigo ya de tu mano la memoria.

Mayo 11–14

Plotters

Toward all the things that draw you here
I am well disposed.
When you name the bread,
the letters, the window, the wall,
the narrow bed,
the pencil with which I talk to you—
even what you mention and it doesn't exist—
I greet them
as if receiving you in your mute presence,
and I go with you on your discovery.
I am your best accomplice.
And so much a plotter am I,
with your ghostly goings-on,
with your sleepwalking visits,
that when, upon your return,
you begin to tell your adventures,
I also join the audience
to hear the story.

May 20

Confabulados

Hacia todas las cosas a las que aquí tú acudes
yo tengo el ademán dispuesto.
Cuando nombras el pan,
las cartas, la ventana, el muro,
la cama angosta,
el lápiz con que te hablo
—hasta lo que mencionas y no existe—,
yo les saludo
como recibiéndote en tu muda presencia,

y te acompaño en su descubrimiento.
Yo soy tu mejor cómplice.
Y tan confabulado estoy
con tus trajines fantasmales,
con tus sonámbulas visitas,
que cuando, a tu regreso,
te pones a contar tus aventuras,
yo me sumo también al auditorio
para enterarme del cuento.

                                            Mayo 20

You in Things

You're becoming anonymous.
You've come with your attributes
into this space
where all things had their place.
With no inhibitions
you arrived,
invading small territories,
supplanting.
You took photos of invisible things
which, on your return, you offered to the world's traffic.
There are now two truths:
the one I bring to bear here in daily sips
and the ambit of your discoveries and rituals
that your music lips
spread through broad latitudes.
Your name has been left
confused in things,
and now you identify yourself with all the objects
that your hands consecrate,
from which it is possible
to baptize you again.

                                        May 25

Tu en las Cosas

Te vas haciendo anónima.
Has entrado con tus atributos
a este espacio
donde todas las cosas disponían de un sitio.
Con desenfado
llegaste,

invadiendo pequeños territorios,
desplazando.
Tomaste fotos de cosas invisibles
que, a tu vuelta, ofrecías al tráfico del mundo.
Hay dos verdades ahora:
la que aquí ejerzo a sorbos diarios,
y el ámbito de tus hallazgos y rituales
que tus labios de música
distribuyen por anchas latitudes.
Se ha quedado tu nombre
confundido en las cosas,
y ahora te identificas con todos los objetos
que tus manos consagran,
desde los cuales es posible
bautizarte de nuevo.

Mayo 25

Presence

> Militiawoman of the sun of this world.
> Longing for honeycombs. My bees
> rush through the pasture of laughter
> inflicting pain: they celebrate masses.
> Juana Rosa

Suddenly
I have stopped in front of time:
the days come down in vain stalactites,
because it's not exactly a tunnel
but it is an emptiness of existence
where everything useless goes rolling to the depths.
It's like that here . . . and it's more than that.
And it can't be understood except with our flesh
thrust into this hollow,
which is cruelty as certain
as flour of anguish for the only food.
Hatred had a face only in this enclosure.
This isn't in the statistics,
or in the hymns.

I am only the outline of a poem
between iron bars and shadow,
a voice that they've tried to strangle
with mutes.

My dear, don't let any other noun
appear
than this honeycomb sought by your bees
for the business of your masses.
"Militiawoman of the sun"
to watch over "essences,"
only when you come in the strophe

is it peopled with infinity,
this "lowest corner of the presences
between four walls."

Your body, shunning contact,
is the space into which fall
the letters of your name,
and time is shattered.

May 18

Presencia

> Miliciana del sol bajo tus tejas.
> Nostalgia de panales. Mis abejas
> se lanzan por el pasto de las risas
> infligiendo dolor: celebran misas.
> Juana Rosa

De súbito
me he parado ante el tiempo:
los días se descuelgan en vanas estalactitas
porque no es exactamente un túnel,
pero sí una oquedad de la existencia
donde todo lo inútil va rodando hacia el fondo.
Aquí es así . . . y es más.
Y no puede entenderse sino con nuestra carne
metida en este hueco,
que es la crueldad tan cierta
como harina de angustia por único alimento.
El odio tuvo rostro sólo en este recinto.
Esto no está en las estadísticas
ni en los himnos.

Yo sólo soy el trazo de un poema
entre hierros y sombra,

una voz que han querido asfixiar
en sordinas.

No permitas, amiga, que se asome
otro sustantivo
que este panal que buscan tus abejas
para el asunto de tus misas.
"Miliciana del sol"
para custodiar "esencias",
sólo cuando tú vienes en la estrofa
se puebla de infinito
este "ínfimo rincón de las presencias
entre cuatro paredes".

Tu cuerpo, hurtado al tacto,
es el espacio donde van cayendo
las letras de tu nombre,
y el tiempo se hace añicos.

                                                                Mayo 18

Compensation

... that wants to be
memorable bread.
        Juana Rosa

Because the truth is that one is
a stretch of time:
the sum that comes from adding time to time.
But here, as Malraux said, "time
stops, which goes on elsewhere."
It's life that stops, he meant to say.
And I, within the circle, add:
they subtract life from their sum.
All that one has is that space
between one flash of lightning and another
like two mysterious blows.
But it happens
that they steal from one pieces and pieces of road
and don't restore them, like branches on the tree.
The result of the plundering
is the deepest misery:
the total expression of poverty.

A cripple of life
as poor as zero
was I,
when one day you held out your poem to me
to help me survive from you toward life,
like an extra sum of magic subsidy.
It came in the form of bread, as you say;
as if upon my hand they put
your charity from heaven.

                                    May 23

Recompensa

. . . que quiere ser
pan memorable.
        Juana Rosa

Porque en verdad que uno es
un tramo de tiempo:
la cifra que resulta de sumar tiempo y tiempo.
Pero aquí, como dijo Malraux, "se detiene
el tiempo, que continúa en otra parte".
Se detiene la vida, quiso decir.
Y yo, dentro del círculo, agrego;
le restan de su cifra a la vida.
Todo lo que uno tiene es ese espacio
entre relámpago y relámpago
como dos golpes de misterio.
Pero sucede
que le roban a uno pedazos y pedazos de camino
que no se restituyen como las ramas al árbol.
El resultado del despojo
es la mayor miseria:
la total expresión de la pobreza.

Mutilado de vida,
tan pobre como cero
era yo,
cuando un día me acercaste tu poema
para sobrevivirme desde ti hacia la vida,
como una cifra extra de mágico subsidio.
Vino en forma de pan, como tú dices;
como si sobre la mano me pusieran
tu limosna de cielo.

                                        Mayo 23

Repeated Scene

> exiled from the other
>   (from a shoreless love)
> exiled from being
>   (from an open brotherhood)
> still
> exiled from the dream
>   *Juana Rosa*

I've spent so much time
looking at life from here
that it seems the world is split,
that they've cut it in two.
And one has become so used to this piece
that he imagines it's the only one that exists.
It's an enclosed body of water
whose circles slowly move inward:
what a stone in the middle of a puddle
they have destined me to be!
An isolated tower at the top of night
fed by a purple grape.
That's all.

(Ah, Segismundo,* I feel your shadow
here like a demon
who seizes me in your name.
I speak your word as if it were my own;
I repeat your monologue
that crashes against the walls
and comes back.

---

*The protagonist of *La vida es sueño* by Pedro Calderón de la Barca (1600–1681).
The play, one of the greatest of Spain's Golden Age, deals with illusion and
reality. Its most famous line, spoken by Segismundo: "La vida es sueño, y los
sueños sueños son" (Life is a dream, and even dreams are a dream).—D.D.W.

I also doubt the reality
of sleep and wakefulness:
some alien hours that I didn't live,
images of another world
that peers out from me at anguish.
There's nothing but this high shadowy hollow,
where time and man are merged.)

But now it's a question of understanding,
of reviewing the signals;
of tossing a bell up into the air,
of becoming as transparent as time
and taking existence as a book.

These names have been written
with letters of blue fire
on pages from the abyss.
Always someone at the tower and at the bars,
with the same questions.
The hands of other men
have always placed him there:
"exiled from being," like the essential shame,
"exiled from the other," which is to deprive him of love.
The reasons that fall off
like leaves from the other autumn,
the motives turning on a setting,
the same one or different,
they do not matter:
under the song of the hours,
under the tall nights of the dew,
under the most naked solitude,
pointed at by a finger in command . . .
a man has always been there
standing at his fate
"exiled from the dream."

June 2–3

Escena Repetida

> desterrados del otro
>   (de un amor sin orillas)
> desterrados del ser
>   (de una hermandad abierta)
> todavía
> desterrados del sueño
>
>   Juana Rosa

Llevo ya tanto tiempo
mirando desde aquí la vida
que parece que el mundo está partido,
que lo han cortado en dos.
Y tanto se ha acostumbrado uno a este pedazo
que imagina que es lo único que existe.
Es un agua cerrada
cuyos círculos van avanzando hacia dentro:
qué piedra en el centro de un charco
me han destinado ser.
Una torre aislada en lo alto de la noche,
que una uva morada alimenta.
Nada más.

(Ah, Segismundo, siento tu sombra
aquí como un demonio
que me toma en tu nombre.
Hablo tu palabra como propia;
repito tu monólogo
que choca en las paredes
y regresa.
Dudo también la realidad
del sueño y la vigilia:
unas horas ajenas que no viví,
imágenes de otro mundo
que me asoma a la angustia.

No hay más que este alto hueco con sombra,
donde el tiempo y el hombre se confunden.)

Pero se trata ahora de entender,
de repasar los signos;
voltear una campana hacia arriba,
hacerse transparente como el tiempo
y tomar la existencia como un libro.

Con letras de fuego azul se han escrito
estos nombres
sobre páginas del abismo.
Siempre alguien en la torre y las rejas,
con las mismas preguntas.
La mano de otros hombres
lo han puesto siempre allí:
"desterrado del ser", como el oprobio esencial,
"desterrado del otro", que es privarlo de amor.
Las razones que se desprenden
como hojas del otro otoño,
los motivos en turno sobre un escenario,
el mismo o diferente,
no importa:
bajo el canto de las horas,
bajo las altas noches del rocío,
bajo la más desnuda soledad,
señalado por un dedo que ordena . . .
siempre ha estado un hombre allí
parado en su destino,
"desterrado del sueño".

                                        Junio 2–3

Destiny

our letters and poems, and even our relationship,
are obviously for everyone. We are poets . . . not
only so that we can grow but so that the others
can grow.

Juana Rosa

Year after year I've had to witness
time's becoming for me
water flowing uselessly
through a tunnel.
I have felt fall from my chest
April leaves, April leaves,
and from my soul also leaves and leaves.
The aggressions of hatred, anguish with its knots,
untimely white hair,
wounds that will not close their edges,
they have had to be.
This dying of universal deaths
upon a daily moss
has had to be.
This collapse, this evil beneath my name,
has had to be.
This destiny has had to be
so that you might appear
at this well of anguish
and offer your poems
like a grief, that becomes beauty
for the world.

May 27

Destino

nuestras cartas y poemas, y hasta nuestra relación,
son, evidentemente, para todos. Somos poetas . . .
no sólo para crecer nosotros, sino para que
crezcan los demás.

                                        Juana Rosa

He tenido que asistir años y años
a este hacérseme el tiempo
un agua que transcurre inútil
por un túnel.
He sentido caérseme del pecho
hojas y hojas de abril,
y del alma también hojas y hojas.
Ha tenido que ser las agresiones del odio,
la angustia con sus nudos,
las canas a deshora,
las heridas que no unirán sus bordes.
Ha tenido que ser
este morir de universales muertes
sobre un musgo cotidiano.
Ha tenido que ser este derrumbe,
este mal bajo mi nombre.
Ha tenido que ser este destino,
para que tú pudieras asomarte
a ese pozo de angustia
y ofrecer tus poemas
como un dolor que se hace belleza
para el mundo.

                                        Mayo 27

Point of Departure

> It's a time of roots,
> a time to go from sun to tears
> embracing
> the orphan figure of men.
> > *Juana Rosa*

When you arrive like the miracle,
led by hands with a touch of light
and you raise your lamp in the dark,
the dawn comes.
You bring news of life.
In the wake of your passage roads open up.
Simple as a petal on the wind,
you announce a "time of roots"
to save with blows of beauty
"the orphan figure of men."

Dawn's tear smiles at you.

Fairy of words, you
have brought the poem like an archangel's liberating
sword.
To fulfill predictions
I have hastened to your voice that calls
on the other side of the dream.
> > *June 5*

Punto de Partida

> Es tiempo de raíces:
> es tiempo de ir de sol a lágrima
> abrazando
> la huérfana figura de los hombres.
> > *Juana Rosa*

Cuando tú llegas como el milagro,
conducida por manos de un contacto de luz
y alzas tu lámpara en lo oscuro,
amanece.
Traes noticias de la vida.
En la estela de tus pasos van surgiendo caminos.
Ingenua como un pétalo en el viento,
anuncias un "tiempo de raíces"
para salvar a golpes de belleza
"la huérfana figura de los hombres".

La lágrima del alba te sonríe.

Duende tú de palabras,
has traído el poema como espada de arcángel
que libera.
Para cumplir oráculos
he acudido a tu voz que llama
al otro lado del sueño.

                                        Junio 5

Summing Up

> . . . I feel that a series of forces, which were once
> scattered, now converge on the same place.
> . . . It's so fantastic that it seems to me quite
> natural.
>
> Juana Rosa

Now I think of you.
Now you're in the center of ascending circles.
Now I look for you above the clouds;
I walk around as if in groups of mysteries,
determining your smoky shape:
there is no ultimate watchtower for spying,
because a higher plane always tempts me.
There is an interrogative intensity;
your poems keep falling like leaves,
and it's not from an autumn tree,
it's not from a tree, and it's
only from a hollow of inverted light.

When you began the journey through your nights
toward where I was only
a name,
a distant point of misery,
a verse in the corrosion,
what was there in your eyes,
girl of toys and Sundays,
of abstract fishes,
of keys that flee from the piano,
of sudden vertigo,
from which your shoulders perhaps will not return?
What visionary grape
was squeezing into your eyes a magic juice?

What important madness
was trying to found another universe?

Because I was here, without time;
like a crust of death,
under the earth,
with just a little lamp in the depths
of a fold of shadow;
I, as you said,
next to the splinter of hatred
left by "a jailer's kick."
I was a fierce solitude.
And you arrived one day,
intrusive,
giving other names to things.
Where did you get the meaning
of "bread and tears"
of which this consists?
What heavenly semantics
annointed you with the adequate word?
Founder of an epoch,
colonizing foam
you here installed your ghost:
and it's now a living matter,
a custom now of touch,
an indispensable body with a history.
I now could not
say my name without yours appearing
(even my name comes from your lips).
You are so familiar to me
that I begin to relive moments . . . that we never lived.

I'm gradually adding up fragments,
mirages,

I line up seaweed in the sea
and your loving feet go passing over islands,
your breasts of incense,
your hips of magnetized crystal
beneath the cosmos,
the friendship of your hands with keys
and that starry sweat
that drops from your forehead.
Around you
swing the "forces that converge on one place"
where you trace a sign.
You say it
raising your lips of night dew
like a kiss of music.
You have the apostolic faith of song
and you cross crumbling strophes
like star petals.

From my broken life,
from this sum of ashes
with a still hidden flame,
from the vital cyst at whose center still beats
fresh madness,
greens nameless,
assets . . .
I've seen the signs
and, drunk with rebirths,
I break the shell,
I wake my hallucinated other one,
a Lazarus that I raise up and set walking . . .
and I take you by the waist, partner.
From your ceremonial body
I embrace night's friendship.
I pronounce "the word" with your accent,

"as if I did not exist,"
erasing myself
from this "time present,"
and we go from the ancient fountain
up to your transparent house
with coals of dream;
the ritual is all the love of the universe,
there is a ringing of bells,
vertigo is "quite natural";
we have a comet's orbit in our hands;
before our eyes
"a chaliced territory" is held out to us,
ahead.

(In the distance
the "sea behind bars"
is slowly left behind.)*

                                          May 20

Resumen

> . . . siento que una serie de fuerzas, que antes
> estaban dispersas, convergen ahora en el
> mismo lugar.
> . . . Es tan fantástico, que me parece lo más
> natural.
>
>   Juana Rosa

Ahora te pienso.
Ahora estás tú en el centro de círculos que ascienden.
Ahora te busco nieblas arriba;

---

*Soon after finishing A Correspondence of Poems, Angel Cuadra was transferred to
the island's maximum security jail.—J.R.P.

ando como en categorías de misterios,
precisando tu forma de humo:
no hay atalaya última para atisbar,
porque siempre un plano más arriba me tienta.
Hay una intensidad interrogante;
van cayendo como hojas tus poemas,
y no es de un árbol del otoño,
y no es de un árbol, y no es
sino de un hueco de luz a la inversa.

Cuando iniciaste el viaje por tus noches
hacia donde yo era sólo
un nombre,
un punto de miseria lejano,
un verso en el óxido,
¿qué había en tus pupilas,
muchacha de juguetes y domingos,
de peces abstractos,
de teclas que se fugan del piano,
de vértigo súbito
desde donde tus hombros acaso no regresen?
¿Qué uva visionaria
exprimía en tus ojos un zumo mágico?
¿Qué locura importante
intentaba fundar otro universo?

Porque yo estaba aquí, sin tiempo;
como un mendrugo de muerte,
bajo tierra,
sólo con una lamparita en lo hondo
de un pliegue de sombra;
y, como tú dijiste,
junto a la astilla de odio
que dejó el "puntapié de un carcelero".

Era yo una feroz soledad.
Y tú llegaste un día,
intrusa,
poniéndole otros nombres a las cosas.
¿Desde dónde traías el sentido
de "pan y lágrimas"
en que esto consiste?
¿Qué celeste semántica
te ungió con la adecuada palabra?
Fundadora de un tiempo,
colonizando espumas
instalaste tu fantasma aquí:
y ya es asunto vivo,
costumbre ya del tacto,
imprescindible cuerpo con historia.
Ya no podría
decir mi nombre sin que el tuyo aparezca
(hasta mi nombre viene de tus labios).
Me eres tan conocida
que me pongo a repasar momentos . . . que no tuvimos.

Voy sumando retazos,
espejismos,
pongo algas en fila en el mar
y van pasando tus pies de amor sobre islas,
tus senos de incienso,
tus caderas de imantados cristales
bajo el cosmos,
la amistad de tus manos con llaves
y ese sudor de estrellas
que en tu frente resbala.
En torno tuyo
giran "las fuerzas que convergen en un lugar"
donde tú trazas un signo.

Tú lo dices
empinando tus labios de relente
como un beso de música.
Tienes la fe apostólica del canto
y cruzas desmenuzando estrofas
como pétalos de astros.

Desde mi vida rota,
desde esta suma de cenizas
con una llama aún oculta,
desde el quiste vital en cuyo centro aún late
fresca locura,
verdes anónimos,
posibles . . .
he visto las señales
y, ebrio de renacencias,
rompo la cáscara,
despierto a mi otro alucinado,
Lázaro que levanto y echo a andar . . .
y te tomo del talle, compañera.
Desde tu cuerpo ceremonial
abrazo la amistad de la noche.
Pronuncio "la palabra" con tu acento,
"como si yo no fuera",
borrándome
de este "tiempo de aquí",
y andamos desde la fuente antigua
hasta tu casa transparente
con carbones de sueño;
el rito es todo el amor del universo,
hay campanas,
el vértigo es "lo más natural";
tenemos la órbita de un cometa en las manos;
ante los ojos

"un territorio cáliz" se nos tiende,
adelante.

(A lo lejos
el "mar entre rejas"
se va quedando atrás.)

                                                        Mayo 20

A New Deuteronomy

To help me to survive from you toward
life like an extra sum of magic subsidy.
                              Angel

Your voice speaks the grief of our clay
shattered in the shadow,
giving light through the millenary wound.
Here the reality. Off there the dreams.
Our cup who art in history,
split in two, and the sea
swelling in your center,
you now achieve a crystal transparency.

In cold calculation, and all the rest,
for God's pulse trembled,
any embrace we give each other
will be outside the limits
of the somnivorous gods: let joy
be as it may,
our people lifting their lips,
within so many centuries.

The fountain mystifies itself with its keys.
The world's new law
will be written in cyclical sands
with lights escaped from the depths
of the tasted pardon of our wine.
The "magic subsidy" of the dawn:
two voices facing the sun
and a single true rhythm.
                              Juana Rosa
                    Miami, August 6, 1979

Nuevo Deuteronomio

> para sobrevivirme desde ti hacia la vida
> como una cifra extra de mágico subsidio.
> *Angel*

Tu voz dice el dolor del barro nuestro
escindido en la sombra,
dando luz por la herida milenaria.
Aquí la realidad. Allá los sueños.
Vaso nuestro que estás en la historia
partido en dos, y el mar
creciéndote en el centro,
ya ganas transparencia de cristal.

Considerando en frío, y todo lo demás
que a Dios le tembló el pulso,
abrazo que nos demos
será fuera del ámbito
de los dioses somnívoros: seráse
que seráse la alegría,
empinando los labios nuestro pueblo,
dentro de tantos siglos.

La fuente se enmisteria con sus llaves.
La nueva ley del mundo
estará escrita en cíclicas arenas,
con escapadas luces desde el fondo
del gustado perdón de nuestro vino.
El "mágico subsidio" de la aurora:
dos voces cara al sol
y un solo ritmo verdadero.

Juana Rosa
Miami, agosto 6, 1979

Juana Rosa Pita was born in Havana on 8 December 1939 and left Cuba in 1961. In 1975 she won first prize for Hispanic-American poetry from the Instituto de Cultura Hispánica de Málaga (Spain). Between 1976 and 1986 she headed Solar poetry publications (Washington, Miami, Boston), where her first books appeared. Awarded two international prizes in Italy, the Ultimo Novecento of Pisa (1985) and the Alghero "Culture for Peace" (1987), her poetic work has been extensively reviewed and has been translated into English, Italian, and German. Among her fifteen published books are *Pan de sol* (Washington: Solar, 1976), *Manual de magia* (Barcelona: Ambito Literario, 1979), *Viajes de Penélope* and *Crónicas del Caribe* (Washington: Solar, 1980 and 1983), *Plaza sitiada* (San José, Costa Rica: Libro Libre, 1987), and *Florencia nuestra* (Miami: Arcos, 1992). She was Visiting Professor at Tulane University, New Orleans, between 1990 and 1992. With the book of poems *Una estación en tren* (North South Center, University of Miami, forthcoming), she won the Letras de Oro prize for 1992–93. About her poetry, the Nicaraguan poet Pablo Antonio Cuadra has written, "Book by book Juana Rosa Pita is building a mysterious realm of love and prophecy: an enchanted isle where the word restores what hate turned to ashes" ("Poetas de América," *La Prensa Literaria*, Managua, 12 December 1982).

The poems that in 1979 would inspire Angel Cuadra's *Poemas en correspondencia (desde prisión)* [*A Correspondence of Poems (from Jail)*] belong to Pita's second and third books, five from *Las cartas y las horas* (Solar, 1977), written in 1975, and ten from *Mar entre rejas* (Solar, 1977), written in the fall of 1976 immediately after she received Angel Cuadra's first letter. The poems published in *Mar* drew an immediate response: ". . . an elegy of a lost freedom and a song to human freedom" (Antonio Chazarro Montiel, *La Estafeta Literaria*, Madrid, 15 December 1977). ". . . a fundamental book in Cuban contemporary poetry. Juana Rosa Pita makes her very own the tragic life experience of the poet in jail, and turns it into something intimate and personal . . . a poetic resultant of Cuban

Prize-winning poet Juana Rosa Pita in the 1970s.

historical reality . . . the unity established between the poet and the poetic subject is a spiritual hymn, an ever rising process flowing into a mystical contemplation of freedom" (Matias and Yara Montes, Congress of Feminine Writers, Ottawa, May 1978). The poems of Las cartas, translated by Donald Walsh, were included in New Directions in Prose and Poetry 49 (New York, 1985).

Brief Letter to Donald Walsh
Translator of My Poems (in Memoriam)

Angel Cuadra

My friend:
In what language shall we begin our conversation?
How can I begin to celebrate
the support your voice gives me
in sending out my songs, drenched in your accents,
to live in this world?
And not know what the warmth of your hand is like
                in friendship;
only this music shining from the soul,
stretching like a bridge between us:
you in your country open to the stars,
I behind bars of rancor,
dying since the dawn.
Yet even so we meet.
The hands of friends
brought your name to me with the morning dew.
And you are here, and I am talking to you.

Because I've learned that not everything is hatred.
I want to declare another word,
sow it as it were in furrows
of goodness and of hope.

There are some men who crush my words,
tear me to pieces for producing beauty,

bring my poem to trial
and sentence it to run the gauntlet:
the drops of blood my poem sheds
form a constellation among the stars.

But there are other men who rescue me
and save my poem like unransomed light,
who gather up its pieces of suffering clay
and, like Prometheus, lend me fire for it.
The fire of love, I proclaim it now,
that is the word I will defend
in martyrdom, among the thorns.
My poem, the grape of pain
for which I bleed and grow.

And you exist, Donald Walsh.
I knew nothing of your musical being,
of that gemstone clear and high, transparent.
Don't leave now
that I have found days dawning in my heart
that were sent me by your hand.
Don't leave now
that we begin to speak in a language
that unites the souls of Whitman and Martí.
And on the streets of all the world
—without bars, without bitterness or fear
—you and I will walk together, speaking
the word of Love that has existed since before the age
    of man.

Angel Cuadra
22/III/80, Boniato Prison

[Donald Walsh died a few days before the arrival of this poem, which was
enclosed in a letter from Cuadra written in April 1980. Translation by
Catherine Rodríguez-Nieto.]

Carta Mínima a Donald Walsh, Traductor de Mis Versos (in Memoriam)

Amigo:
¿En qué idioma comenzaremos el diálogo?
¿Cómo ponerme a celebrar
ese apoyo que me ofrece tu voz
para lanzar mis cantos, mojados de tu acento,
a vivir en el mundo?
Y no saber cómo es el calor de tu mano en el afecto;
sólo esta irradiación de música del alma
tendida como un puente:
tú en tu país abierto a las estrellas,
yo entre rejas de rencor
muriendo desde el alba.
Y aun así nuestro encuentro.
Manos amigas,
con el rocío me enviaron tu nombre.
Y estás aquí, y te hablo.

Porque he aprendido que no todo es el odio.
Quiero afirmar otra palabra,
sembrarla como en surcos
de bien, de esperanzas.

Unos hombres me estrujan las palabras,
me despedazan por hacer la belleza,
colocan mi poema ante los jueces

y le dan con el látigo y el látigo:
la sangre que el poema vierte
se hace constelación arriba, en las estrellas.

Pero otros hombres me rescatan;
me salvan el poema como la luz irredenta;
recogen sus pedazos de barro doloroso
y, prometeicamente, me le prestan el fuego.
Fuego de amor—proclamo—,
que es la palabra que defiendo
entre las espinas y el martirio.
Poema mío, uva de dolor,
por la que sangro y crezco.

Tú existes Donald Walsh.
Yo no sabía de tu ser musical,
de piedra clara y transparente y alta.
No te vayas ahora,
que he descubierto auroras en mi pecho
que vienen de tu mano.
No te vayas ahora
que empezamos a hablar en un idioma
en donde Whitman y Martí se anudan.
Y en las calles del mundo
—sin rejas, sin rencores, sin miedos—
vamos a andar hablando
la palabra de Amor que es anterior al hombre.

Angel Cuadra
22/III/80, Cárcel de Boniato

Yesteryear's Lost Hope: Selections from the UNARE Underground Essay and Poems (1963)

The UNARE Essay

[The following essay (originally entitled "La poesía Cubana frente al comunism: ensayo histórico-literario") is a long, dense statement of the reasons for the UNARE organization's opposition to Castro communism. It includes a lengthy summary of Cuban history from colonial times to the Castro period. I have condensed and edited this part of the essay to the bare essentials.—Ed.]

Literary production is generally conditioned by the time and place in which it is produced. The artist is a witness to his historic moment, the child of a country in which he was fated to live, the antenna of a social ambiance gravitating upon his existence. Poetry, one of the most difficult expressions of Art, is perhaps the most propitious for receiving those vibrations, reflecting life forms and the deepest nerve of the time it is produced. It is the purpose of this preface to present a broad picture of Cuban poetry during the course of this century, but with a special effort to note the relations, the correspondences, of our poetry with the different historical stages and the political and social circumstances of our country.

The Spanish dominion of our Island having ended after thirty years of heroic struggle, our nation was unable to exercise the immediate sovereignty of a country that had won its freedom in legendary strokes. The participation of the United States in the war against Spain on our soil produced the American occupation and intervention of the country and therefore a train of events and a development of later circumstances well different from those projected by the men who led the War of 1895. Then, when nearly four years after the end of the [Spanish-American] war the Republic is established in 1902, it is under [an American-inspired] repression of popular [Cuban] will for the sake of a compromise that favored the maintenance of social and economic structures similar to those of the colony. Now absent from the national scene were the guides of the revolution—Martí, Maceo, and Calixto García dead, and Máximo Gómez shunted to one side. The country having been ravaged by war, our economy was oriented toward dependence on foreign capital.

At the turn of the century our poetry is in disarray. Our great precursors of Modernismo Julián del Casal and José Martí were dead. The same fate befell two young poets of true promise: Juana Borrero and Carlos Pío Uhrbach, the latter fallen in the field of battle of the War of Independence. Some outstanding figures were indeed left, but they came from the colonial period, such as Federico Uhrbach and Bonifacio Byrne. But they do not mark paths to be followed by the next poetic wave of the century's first decade. Byrne, however, is able to sound the tocsin of disenchantment after the Cuban struggle in his poem Mi Bandera (My flag), as he beholds the fatherland on his return from exile:

On my return from a distant strand,
My soul somber and in mourning thrown,
Eagerly sought I my flag
And found another beside my own.
With a faith to austere souls bestown,
Today with profound zeal hold I
That two flags must not fly
Where one is quite enough: my own.

Indeed the first ten years of our life as a republic offer a poetry without great transcendence. Prevalent are the influences of end-

of-the-century Spanish poets, decadent romanticism, some fore-
shadowings of *Modernismo*. There is a tendency toward rotund
versification and a declamatory tone. Some patriotic poetry is
written recounting heroic deeds and figures of the war; motifs
from the Cuban landscape with its creole picturesqueness; and
the influences in some of the styles of Julián del Casal.

[A summary of the next sixteen pages follows in italic type.]

*True to the dictum that a national poetry is not only conditioned by the time
and place that it is produced but that to be authentic it should also reflect the
deepest social, economic and political preoccupations of its time, the writer at
this point explores the state of Cuban poetry during the first three decades of
the republic, culminating in the 1933 revolution against the president-turned-
dictator Gerardo Machado. A most interesting and telling point connected with
the Machado revolution is the treachery of the Cuban Communist Party when
it struck a deal with the dictator, as it would later with General Batista,
supporting his first presidency.*

*Following the anti–President Machado revolt of 1933 and into the first
Batista presidency of 1940–44, Cuban poetry (aside from black poetry and
made-to-order communist verse) split into two general currents. The first consisted of a mainstream whose works were permeated with earlier European
vanguardisms acclimated to the Cuban milieu. Within that framework, however, there was a return to more direct forms of expression not disconnected
from logic, seeking human values and proclaiming the importance of life. These
poets did not band together; they did not form schools or cluster about literary
magazines. Many of them would be influenced by the Chilean Pablo Neruda,
as were Guillermo Villarronda and the neoromantic José Angel Buesa.*

*Secondly, there was an altogether intellectual current, which may be summed
up as art for art's sake. Starting about 1939, this group ignored the vulgar
majority and jettisoned from their poetry all traditional aesthetic, logical, anec-
dotal, social, and historical elements, leaving only highly distilled essences, a
literary path remindful of Ortega y Gasset's observations in "The Dehuman-
ization of Art." These poets turned their backs disdainfully on the politics of
the post-Machado era [1933–53], the vying for power and public favor among
Batista, Auténtico, Communist, and conservative factions. They congregated*

about the figure of José Lezama Lima, author later in the early Castro years of the celebrated novel Paradiso.

The 10th of March coup d'état is produced in 1952, enthroning in our native land a new—worse—Fulgencia Batista dictatorship. How does that unfortunate event affect us? Concerning the state of mind of the citizenry, we have already broadly sketched the general disenchantment. Concerning the intellectual and, specifically, the poetic climate, the two [existing] poetic directions were followed by a new generation of poets just coming of age at the time of the military coup and the approaching revolutionary process.

New literary generations are always guided inspirationally by the previous; they form themselves in the latter's mold; from their wellspring they glean structuring ingredients. Only one or two figures of a rising generation do from time to time break that kind of given idiosyncracy and thrust toward the future, sweeping away the sediments. Thus the younger poets of this period either formed themselves in the first direction pointed out—that of a clearer and more direct poetic expression, in closer touch with the human, accessible to literary polemics even though isolated and individualistic—or they formed themselves in the fascination and extravagance of the poets of the magazine *Orígenes*; their attitudes and poetic materials they adopted from the latter's quarry. Regardless of the mutations attempted by any of the new poets, their starting point would always be along the [former generation's] general lines.

Lacking that uneasiness, that revisionary attitude of refocusing the national problematic, that ideological ferment, that cultural background gained by the struggle against Machado; lacking the collective conscience of a previous process and with the spirit of the citizenry mottled by the grey dust of disenchantment, our people undertook the fight against the Batista dictatorship.

After fruitless efforts at political solutions attempted by national figures and civic institutions, the path was closed to a peaceful solution of the crisis. Direct action was begun by means of an armed underground struggle. The motives that impelled us were the offense to national dignity by the betrayal of the military and, consequently, the desire to rescue our freedom. Our goal was to bring down Batista. The struggle was more of action than of thought. What was being fought against was known, but what we were fighting for was not defined. The organizations mainly heading the fray were the 26th of July Movement [Castro], the 13th of March Revolutionary [student] Directorate, and the organizations formed by the members of the overthrown Auténtico party. A guerrilla war broke out in the mountains and underground action groups were organized. . . . The corruption of Batista's government, the lack of backing by his "armed forces" in the final moments, and the ever more heated fight, among other reasons, were to determine the tyrant's flight on January 1, 1959, and the completion of a prior process, perhaps unique up to the present, in the history of Latin America.

But, what had we prepared for the hour of victory? Here was the opportunity, at last, of applying a solution to the evils of the republic and restructuring the nation toward true democracy by organizing national life with a deep transformation in the political, social, and economic aspects. But again we lacked our often mentioned "cohesion in ideology and program." No program of things to do at the hour of victory was produced during the struggle. It was the most brilliant opportunity in our history, since it was a victorious revolution without any obligations but to itself and to the destiny of the Cuban people. There were indeed some outlines of a program, such as the Sierra Maestra proclamation, whose simple and ineffectual plan did not even come through as a battle standard. On the contrary, it was cast into a complete void by the revolutionary leadership which became embodied in one man. The blight of *caudillismo*—a chronic evil in our Hispanic America—was re-edited in Cuba with fatal consequences.

Lacking a program, the destiny of the country was left to the improvisations and madnesses of the revolutionary *caudillo*. The only ones who knew where they were headed and what they wanted were the Communists, who had done little or nearly nothing in the revolution and whose cadres returned to the country after a comfortable exile subsidized by international communism. Little by little the leaders who fought the revolution were replaced, imprisoned, or shot. Communism kept gaining ground and sole leader Fidel Castro changed the objectives of the revolution by traitorously turning over the fatherland's destiny to Soviet communism. From what the immense majority of the people and the men who fought expected to what the Revolution turned out to be, there was a distance that can only be expressed by "Foiled again!"

During the period of resistance against Batista, poetry was not—as it was not against Machado—a true weapon, organized and constant so as to be a notable, significant fact in our literary history. As we pointed out, the rising young poets followed one or the other of the two currents preceding the dictatorship; they did not create a militant revolutionary poetry bent to a specific purpose. Those who followed the currents of the Orígenes group owing to their schooling and idiosyncrasy, or owing to the poetic idiom in which they had modulated their voices, contributed nothing at all. The most inclined to opposition were those that followed the other line, since their poetry was more direct, more in touch with humanity, because their attitude— more distant from the ivory tower—placed them in possession of the means of producing a civil poetry that would sing in an idiom closer to the collective taste and sensibility, the events, the facts, the tragedy of the moment. It required a turning outward for a meeting with the masses and with surrounding objective reality.

It would be unfair to say that nothing was done; within this aesthetic line mainly, revolutionary poetry was produced and even printed in publications, in the newspapers in which the Batista dictatorship permitted, now and then, an opinion from the press. It circulated in the underground at the rawest of times and was published abroad. We could even make a brief summary of those scattered works. We could point out voices like Pura del Prado's, long since absent from the country. We could point out characteristics and reproduce verses. But we shall not; the poetic results did not transcend; the period is very recent. Many of those who wrote against the dictatorship at that stage, so scattered in style literarily, later went off in different directions from those suiting our purpose. But what we wish to refer to, the object of this study, is that no school or group of poets gained cohesion under a political or revolutionary militancy with the specific intention of creating a poetic opposition, under the ideological discipline of an organization, to the dictatorship that the Cuban people opposed.

In what follows this preface, we shall have to keep names in silence, because this writing that now sees the light of day is being done at these moments of a fierce and inhuman dictatorship that holds in its power the life and liberty of its mildest opponent. In the guise of a prior listing that will clarify conclusions of this study, the Cuban poets in the epoch of the communist empire in this country may well be differentiated in four groups, such as were noted in a lecture on "Cuban Literature under Communism" given at the Círculo Hispanoamericano of Atlanta, U.S.A., by the North American professor Wilder P. Scott: (1) those who were always communists; (2) those who have later joined ruling communism; (3) those who have taken the path of exile; (4) those who stand up within the country to the oppressive regime by writing against it.

And if it is impossible to identify those who make up the fourth aspect for the danger to their lives, it is just as fair, save for rare exceptions, not to identify either those who belong to the other three classifications.

In the state of affairs previously described, the triumph of the 1959 Revolution takes our poetry by surprise. Popular emotion pulled all the stops in its support of the triumphant upheaval.

Everywhere was a desire to support; for some, to seize the opportunity. It was a matter of collaborating, of contributing ideas, projects, indeed of improvising "at the hour of victory," as José Martí asserted, the harvest that was not sown "at the hour of war." Thus was it too with culture and art and so it happened—when the communists had not yet assumed the power that the *caudillo* was to hand them—that the official vehicles of cultural transmission fell into the hands precisely of those who were formed poetically in the hermetic, surrealist, escapist, obscure Baroque current . . . of the poets of Orígenes and others of similar aesthetic and human directions.

They belonged chronologically to the generation that was already there (men about thirty years of age), and under their direction the first art magazine was published: *Lunes de Revolución*. They provided the initial keynote. But they found themselves with the difficult task of producing a more direct, more with-the-people poetry to sing and to reflect the objective and immediate reality; and for this they were not suited intellectually and aesthetically. Of course they made an effort to readapt; they improvised in an effort to find the formula to take them to their particular abstract modes on their way to the concrete, from the subjective to the objective, from escape to a meeting with the multitude. We may qualify the result as literary hybridism. This is a fact they cannot deny. Even the communist writer José Antonio Portuondo, in his sectarian *Bosquejo Histórica de las Letras Cubanas* (1960), referring to the moments of existence of said magazine, confesses that it sprang from "the confusion of some youths" who were trying (he failed to call it what it really was) "to make out of surrealist or abstractionist forms—simple pathways of escape of hoary reactionary origin—*impossible* aesthetic instruments for the new revolutionary spirit." This statement should be amplified to a confession that it was the beginning of the result of opportunism, bastardy, a lack of scruples and dignity that in all the orders of human events has flowed toward the den of wickedness that communism has made of our national life.

At the final stage the communists assumed all the controls, consequently including those of culture. All that was necessary was a call to collaborators through the formation of organizations which, in the artistic field, culminated in the Unión Nacional de Escritores y Artistas de Cuba (the National Union of Writers and Artists of Cuba), UNEAC, to which flowed poets from various aesthetic directions. And, under the directorship of the old-line communists—on their way back to a power handed to them—came together surrealists, abstractionists, followers of the *Orígenes* formulas, neoromantics, eclectics, popular balladeers and peasants, all blending into an eager chorus of literary compromise, demanding a poetry that should try, according to them, to reach the fiber and the understanding not of the people— which is something else—but of the masses, which, turned into an ever baser rabble, sing slogans to the *caudillo* in the public square. More disgraceful is this yet when, among these official poets, there are those of undeniable poetic talent. As a result a level of absurdity—not to say mockery—was reached wherein a "poetry workshop," or something to that effect, was created to crank out slogans in verse. An exhibit mural of poems was organized with motifs or themes, nearly all of them of the communist revolution. In it poetic defamation assumes the aspect of a paid blurb. Besides the latter's low quality, it manifests a confusion of means, styles and projections which, by sounding the keynote of the current officially patronized poetic moment, places future Cuban poetry at this base wellspring where many youths of the up-and-coming generation run the risk of poetic malnutrition.

The objectives of the revolution having been negated, our people once again are witness to the spectacle of a frustration now more baffling than ever, since a fierce and foreign ideology takes over the government, imposing a dictatorship joined by rabid and vindictive fanatics; thus an atmosphere of discord in social as well as in family life, causing a separation among Cubans by hate, desolately, under the claw of terror. The fight begins all over again: an effort on the part of the same men who bore on their shoulders the weight of anti-Batista revolutionary travail; and it is upon this weariness alas that they attempt to renew strength and energy. Now numerous dispersed anti-communist organizations are being created. The intention is to use the same tactics employed against Batista. The bottom line is the rescue of the Cuban Revolution that slipped through the very hands of those who set its course. It is the same inner turmoil that since the War of 1895 has run invisibly, stinging through national conscience and aspiration. Still, in spite of it all it has not congealed inwardly into a definite and definitive state of conscience. There are those bereft of their former economic and social privileges who see in the anti-communist struggle merely the means perhaps of restoring what is lost or will soon be lost. Then there are the comrades in the revolutionary struggle who feel betrayed but are too overwhelmed, most of them, to understand that neither in the tactics they used before will they achieve victory, nor in the lukewarm formulas of a return to the timeworn "institutional normality" will there be a cohesive strength to unite wills.

Thus these revolutionary forces, far from uniting, have scattered and proliferated in groups that again will to oppose something but without deciding what to favor. In the face of an ideology it is indispensable to formulate the objectives of the battle to oppose it. The underground struggle and guerrilla warfare in the mountains now break out afresh. The extraordinary military aid contributed by Russia to our oppressors to repress the growing opposition, plus the old "reasons for rebellion" now surfacing that were never the object of worry of the rulers and the powerful during our republican existence, are now producing an outcome of adhesion to the fanatic [Cuban] communist political credo, the actualizer of hidden passions and hate. The abandonment in which those opposing communism find themselves without outside help from any country to carry out the fight, including the United States, besides so many other reasons, has caused defeat after defeat for the nearly defenseless democratic forces that are beginning to fight all over again.

Terror presently unleashes its sway. The jails are replete with thousands of Cubans; forced labor concentration camps are created; hundreds of Cubans are executed without letup before the firing squad; thousands flee to exile, causing the greatest exodus in the memory of America. Official propaganda is oppressive; foreign communism is force-fed in massive doses. Life's vision slips by through an imposed, solitary viewpoint. There is poverty, betrayal, terror and hate. The landscape is blurred, the climate leaden, the atmosphere smothering. Government directives and orders now arrive from Moscow. Next to the Cuban flag flies the Soviet. What prospects does poetry now offer? Especially, what is in store for it? Given the models tailored by the officially prescribed poetry as the wellspring of the new poetic generation, the perspective is alarming. In the poetic hybridism we pointed out, now with the cultural mainstream perfectly under communist control, the emerging generation of poets seems to have its path staked out. Our rulers possess all the ingredients to create a generation in their own style: a planned mentality, an artistic production fabricated in their molds.

Yet, for all that, the product has not turned out thus. Art cannot be framed within production goals. The current court poets, ensconced in the Union of Artists and Writers of Cuba, have not manufactured a product of genuine value, nor have they overcome the arrhythmia of hybridism. The youths following the footsteps of the court poets suffer from the disaster produced from the imitation of a dreadful model. Even within the recesses of the Union there exist divisions among groups, produced on the one hand as the result of the phony creation that it is and, on the other, because of differences of aesthetic attitudes that are unalloyable, as well as by ambitions and personal group or poetic caste differences.

But we can point out yet something else. The environment again sets the conditions of literary expression. The climate of fresh disappointment, frustration and sham is decisive; and it is evident in its grey profile under the mantle of lies with which the Union of Writers tries to cover us. Again the equation formed by man and his environment prevails over all the attempts to

belie this eternal struggle, and results similar to past stages we
have traversed begin to dawn upon us. There is not at this point
enough material for definite conclusions, but something begins
to be noticed in the most recent poets. Of those now over twenty
years of age, some have joined the official chorus of pamphleteering poetry in the already described fashion, while others seek,
again, the current of escape from the present environment.

A recent publication titled *Novísima poesía cubana* (Newest Cuban
poetry), published in December 1962, makes a brief summary
of poets "born around 1940 and after who began writing after
the assumption of power by the Revolution." Without making
an overall judgment—a difficult matter because of the dissimi-
larity of those involved and because of their youth, as well as
the concerns that we wish to stress in this study—we observe
in this group of poets the above-mentioned directions. And in
the distance, from their literary commitment or in their sloganeering poetry, the prevailing note is evident. The publication is
headed by a preface with a brief and partial description of the
latest poetry. The work initially focuses on the appearance of the
Orígenes group and after a pale effort to review the ideas outlined
by that group—the genuine products of a period of national
frustration—it ends by declaring: "all experience having been in-
validated, the scale of values having been modified by the social
changes taking place in the country and refusing to drop into
the current defamatory mode, these poets have seen themselves
obliged, in the midst of the thematic vacuum running two years
now, to subscribe to a formal *neo-origenismo*. . . ." It concludes
by affirming that the paths followed lead to "two equally sterile
extremes":

1. a poetry turned into itself, renouncing all communication
and the least objectivity, producing as a reaction,
2. a propagandistic poetry, done for the here and now. Both
extremes are alien to man; they ignore him; the latter because
it depersonifies him, because it considers the circumstances
and not the individual; the former because it deprives him of

his relationships, because it considers the individual without his circumstances.

For all that, there is something else to point out in this regard. The selfsame preface calls attention specifically to the publication of the poem *La marcha de los hurones* (The march of the ferrets), by Isel Rivero, 1960, since then departed from Cuba, who was twenty-two years old at the time. This kind of work is pointed out as of the utmost importance in considering the poets selected, who attempt to typify their generation. The preface, however, tries through justification to duck the responsibility of the selection, perfectly understandable for whoever lives in Cuba today. The poem, of the highest quality among those chosen, offers visions and testimonies such as:

It is urgent for us to labor,
saturated with a bitter resin.
It is urgent to forge ahead, all quest now useless.
Conformity has not been given to us.
Optimism has not been given to us.
We foresee decadence right at birth.
We are damned, but it is inevitable for us to point out now,
in spite of our being annulled,
in spite of our being bound in a thread of uncertainty:
Truth has infinite faces
besides the one we live and die in.
It is impossible to find a collective truth.
They insist on our singing battle hymns,
but history has been repeated
and in some remote corner of a certain day
these pools of blood were already spilled for the same
                                                                          reasons.
To our thousand-year-old hearts
the reclamation of faith is naive.
It is essential, now, that we gather up the bodies
                          of the heroes,

and cleanse their wounds . . .
It is urgent that we end the fairy tale
for the good of the children;
urgent it is that we allow this voice
to filter through the consequences.

This would nearly suffice to understand, behind it all, the basic discouragement, the frustration, the horror, the leaden atmosphere, the grey grimace of present-day Cuban events through the reflection of a segment of our youngest literary generation—dispersed and confused.

We have already outlined superficially the struggle against communism in its first stages in our country, and the hardly adequate procedure of those who once again cast themselves into the fight, disunited and discouraged, and how this attitude contributes to successful repression on the part of the dictatorial regime. The unity of all Cubans is necessary in ideology and program, as Varona pointed out years before.* This disunity was one of the principal causes of the failures of anti-Castro attempts, culminating in the Bay of Pigs disaster, an invasion that did not count on the conscious joint action of the democratic forces inside the country.

Thus, in mid-1961, appears in the midst of the struggle and terror, the Unidad Nacional Revolucionaria (UNARE) which, following the axiom of José Martí that "before being called to war, a people must know what it seeks, where it is going, and what is to come later," brings within its fold men of past revolutionary struggles and fresh spirits adhering to an ideology and a program, all in all, the program of the New State, which, to the amazement of many, begins to move through all corners of the underground with the object of carrying into the struggle the ideological content that heretofore that struggle lacked. Thus the program pos-

---

*Enrique José Varona (1849–1933), noted essayist, patriot, poet, and literary critic.

tulates: "History indeed shows that where more than sufficient heroism has been present but the ideological content missing, reactionary forces, concealed and indifferent during the struggle for freedom, take over the state and avail themselves of the sacrifice of others. That is the cause of the failure of the Revolution that culminated the First of January 1959 and which has degenerated traitorously into a bloody joke on the Cuban people.

"The lack of an ideological instrument to challenge with philosophic reasoning his Marxist-Leninist sophistries leads Fidel to exult, from on high in his Caesarist pulpit, imputing to his adversaries an absence of political, social and economic principles. Thus the silence of the opposition to his challenge is interpreted by the masses as the truth of his brash assertions."

The question is not one of issuing a simple proclamation, nor of an ambiguous program allowing for twisted or equivocal interpretations of its general axioms with room enough to diminish the value or betray again the goals of the struggle. Our program is based on reaping all the experience of the Republic's life, whose ills were never resolved with the application of an abstract democracy that, in the midst of politics, militarism, administrative corruption and the tragedy of *caudillismo*, never solved the Cuban problem in a basic way politically, socially and economically, as the country swung between restlessness and disenchantment. The question is based on the study of our environment as well as of our Latin American reality, and of the current circumstances of international relations as well as of our history, succession of periods and events. It is furthermore based on its own philosophy of the State, Economy, and Politics, with a novel and acute penetration that ends in a definite political position. It goes toward the rescue of spirituality over materialism; it goes along the paths of Christian and Western idiosyncrasy. It defines without ambiguity what it proposes to do with each aspect of our national life. It is, in sum, a true doctrine that being for all is for no one in particular and thus points the way for men to follow ideals and not *caudillos*; and through its general principles and specific concretions, it marks the clean road for the creation of a national conscience because, finally, this New State, like all social and political states, will need a new man: the citizen without the today and yesterday who will rescue and guard our national dignity. Thus we begin the creation of a man of action who will not go to the fight for the sake of the fight itself but who, like Roberto Arias—one of the most extraordinary leaders of the struggle in Cuba at this stage—upon rising up in arms in the mountains, did so in these words: "With the rifle in one hand and the Program in the other." A man of thought, who with the zeal of a man of action, goes out in search of the people, at the risk of a struggle, which, in the poet, as in the specific case of this essay, uses poetry as a weapon, under one political will and one political conscience.

This latest stage of anti-communist opposition within the country after 1961 is undoubtedly strengthened by the appearance of the Unidad Nacional Revolucionaria. Absolutely no one can ever separate from these terrible days for the fatherland the presence of this organization and its doctrine, ever larger and deeper, which has surpassed the borders of the Island, to gain fertile roots among Cuban emigrés. Just as, in the face of danger the dire need of a cohesive vehicle produced in many fighting men the need of agreeing with the Program of the New State, which brings with it a stimulating breath that, like a warm breeze, speeds throughout the far corners of the underground; now, in the face of that danger, this climate full of hope leads many poets to join in, to come together to support the cause, to unite the weapons of their poetry in a common purpose, reacting in such a way that their means of expression will be conditioned to reflect in their poems the current historical moment and its social reality.

Thus the work of the poets herein represented; theirs is not an artistic approach to a literary aspiration; their purpose is not the setting of aesthetic guidelines for the poetic production of the country, nor is it a generational consequence. It is the "necessity of coincidence" to which our program speaks in reaction to an environment. These are poems with a difference in the formal and stylistic sense, but they have a thematic unity knotting them together with the thread of an objective, patriotic human interest. These are the poets who have embraced National Revolutionary Unity (UNARE).

A fundamental difference exists between these poets and those in the *Novísima poesía cubana* anthology. The work of the latter is the product of the confusion that a state of dispersion produces in them. They come into a baffling world and appear not to take stock of it. As if by intuition they seem to try to seek mankind within the surrounding mists. Those who do not join the official chorus waver between questioning and giving in. To the challenge that objective reality hurls at them they respond generally with an evasive reaction, returning to the cryptic solutions of the past poets of *Orígenes*. We cannot tell—nor can light be shed on this possibility under the present regime—if in later work, now unpublishable, their resulting poetry will be otherwise, stepping through the breach that *The March of the Ferrets* initiated. What we point out herein are the known characteristics of those scattered youths whose poetry the selfsame preface of the book describes as "timid and digressive."

The attitude of the UNARE poets that we bring to light from among the jailhouse walls of today's Cuba is different, as are the purposes and the ends. This is no poetry of hesitation, rather it is of combat. To the challenge that the terrifying ambiance casts at them they fight back. Words become talons, pain is tinged with hope. Theirs is not a crisis of spirit generally, for a certain gesture of hope looks at tomorrow. They do not take refuge in evasive hermetism. Whatever the formal line they take, they always picture the objective reality of the moment they live in. In their words the poets bring their truth of the world they must live in. They do not digress; they have found the mark. They do not write separately; they have taken on one attitude and one political militancy. They have found cohesion in the ideology and the Program of the New State. From this necessity of agreement that we have explained, from this meeting of minds in the ideological, the circumstantial, the historical and human, is this fundamental aesthetic agreement upon a theme to be understood. The work of the poets here collected is as distant from escapism and the ivory tower as it is from sectarianism, sloganeering, and the political pamphlet. Thus it is not a literary stance with its back turned to circumstance, nor is it a compromised art. Nothing compromises these poets if it is not their own will, a will that comes from a sudden sense of duty; a duty imposes on free spirits the patriotism of the children of a country who will not be subjected, of men who are not in conformity with being only witnesses to their time but, rather, who are participants with their verses in the national drama which spurs their senses. Nothing obliges them from the outside; they are sole owners of their artistic environment within which they produce their apolitical work, restricted by nothing. What is here published is born from a state of conscience, a product of factors already noted. It is a spontaneous flow from those who, having found their path, proceed in the knowledge of the way and their responsibility, in the assurance of the flag they embrace. And thus they begin to write on these topics and to interpret their anguish in a manner different from that of the poets who are scattered and misled [by the revolution]. They are different in that they are united in their background [of opposition], which is of major importance for the special transcendence of the school of poetry that is to follow.

The poetical production herein published has been written in Cuba under the terror re-established by the communist regime. It has that in its favor, among other things. The anonymous poets here included face the path tomorrow of imprisonment or emigration, but for now they are here in Cuba, a fact of extraordinary importance. It is the first time that in a country under the communist system a group of intellectuals, of poets, all together under one fighting banner, takes up the spontaneous, voluntary

Angel Cuadra speaking at a Cuban patriotic rally in Ybor City, Tampa, 1990, on the same cigar factory steps from which Martí spoke in 1893. (Editor Warren Hampton is to the right.)

and heroic act of creating a written work directed against the governing regime and generated by actions due to that government. This work stands to be seen by the rest of the world, giving the lie to the fraudulent reality that the system propagandizes tirelessly.

With its control of culture and art and its creation of opportunistic neocourtesan writers slavishly proclaiming the handed down official line, the Cuban communist regime has been able to publish a number of books by its literary choir which they have disseminated in many countries. That poetic production bears the purpose of exporting to other latitudes a picture of Cuban life as planned by the communist power structure. Counter to that version are the poems herein printed and at great risk secretly shipped out, containing their version and denunciation of the true Cuban picture. As José Martí postulated, "each state carries to literature its own expression," and through it, can "the history of nations be told more truly than by its chronicles"; let us leave up to the men and the countries receiving this publication the determination as to which of the two versions proclaims the truth of Cuba today—if in the literary chronicles at the pay of the government, with the pamphleteering poems, or with the poets here presented who, at great risk, offer a work whose expression is the product of the political and social milieu within which it is created.

Few are the poets included here, still with ten men a nation can be founded, said Martí. We shall not judge critically their aesthetic characteristics or their literary aspects. The production here contained we leave to the judgment of those to whose hands it comes, to the judgment of political and literary posterity, to the judgment of the nations receiving its message of underground heroism, and the pain of a people who rise up against the defenselessness and terror that overshadow them as they seek freedom and the definition of their destiny. Other poets will follow in these footsteps. They will be joined by the voices from afar of emigré Cuban poets. And so a state of future conscience shall rise through poetry to provide the life-giving breath to the fatherland. May God grant that the hereafter be the dawn and the freedom that we dream, the future Cuba without the today and the yesterday, the New State perhaps, where we shall not have to grieve, because of futile sacrifice, yet another smothered voice like that of Carlos Pío Uhrbach, dead in the War of 1895, nor shall we have to harken to another voice of discouragement like that of the emigré Bonifacio Byrne, on returning to his country after its independence.

Cuba, May 1964

UNARE's Poetry of Protest: A Sampler

Appended to the original UNARE literary essay was a collection of pseudonymous poems of protest by members of the sub rosa group. The four poems here reproduced include the work of three of five poets: Alejandro Almanza, who is Angel Cuadra; Remigio Palma, who is Carlos Casanova, now living in the United States; and Hatuey del Monte, who is still in Cuba and must remain unidentified.

Introit

The masters of hate,
the new gyrfalcons,
oligarchs in debut,
milkers of mockery,
actors with virulent souls,
executors of ancestral vengeances;
you who in the ears of the people
explode the bombshells of your "social justice";
you, lying microphones,
self-anointed leaders of the poor,

self-appointed captains of the proletariat;
you, cheating messiahs,
hypocritically infuriated;
you, profferers of future honeycombs
with a poisonous reality;
you, technicians of deceit;
you, technicians of insult;
you, technicians of death . . .
you taught us this language I bear.

Alejandro Almanza

Introito

Los señores del odio,
los nuevos gerifaltes,
oligarcas de estreno,
ordeñadores del escarnio,
histriones con el alma virulenta,
albaceas ahora de ancestrales venganzas;
ustedes que en los oídos de los pueblos
estallan los obuses de sus "justicias sociales";
ustedes, microfónicos mentidores,
autoapoderados de los pobres,
autoelegidos capitanes proletarios;
ustedes, encubiertos mesías,
hipócritamente encolerizados;
ustedes, ofrecedores de futuros panales
con realidad de veneno;
ustedes, técnicos del engaño;
ustedes, técnicos del insulto;
ustedes, técnicos de la muerte . . .
ustedes nos enseñaron este idioma que traigo.

Alejandro Almanza

On March 1, 1963, following painful torture sessions, Pedro René Hernández-García, known in the underground struggle by his war name "Roberto Arias," was shot by the Communist tyranny of Cuba. In a heroic gesture for the liberty and the future of the fatherland, he had marched unarmed toward the mountains of Oriente.

The Words of Roberto

He said things like these:
(There was a solidary silence amongst the palms)
That rose and bread ought not to be parted,
that there is a share of joy for all,
and that dreams can indeed obtain.
He said something else that the sea muffled right away.
(There was a solidary silence in the huts.)
I cannot recall, but he shouted nearly like the sun
or a formidable light . . .
He said that man is infinite
and dignity but a lengthy star;
that we shall resurrect.
He said more, much more with his jetstream of blood.
(There was a solidary silence in the dawn moon when they
    shot him.)

                                                     Hatuey del Monte

Palabras de Roberto

Dijo cosas así:
(Había un solidario silencio entre las palmas.)
Que la rosa y el pan no deben separarse,
que la alegría alcanza para todos,
y que se pueden realizar los sueños.

Dijo algo que el mar tapó enseguida.
(Había un solidario silencio en los bohíos.)
No me acuerdo, pero gritaba casi como sol
o formidable luz . . .
Dijo que el hombre es infinito,
y la dignidad sólo una estrella larga;
que resucitaremos.
Dijo más, mucho más con su chorro de sangre.
(Había un solidario silencio en la luna del alba cuando lo
    fusilaron.)

Hatuey del Monte

A Night, Cuba 1963

The city lies outspread
under a night of ancestral writers.

A tropic of big fish
and sunsoaked skin.

A stage for electric needle-fish,
the Island is a testimonial of fire and growth.

Here, Cuba, among flags,
shaken by hymns and fish scales.

Under gray greasepaint, under thick face powder,
the city bears an awesome visage.

During the daylight thundered the parades
of cannon at rest and bullets at attention.

Men of stern mien marched
with geometric expression.

The laughter of children strolled
like rows in waving fields of wheat.

Roundabout prevailed labor union joy,
waves of placards and sloganeering songs.

White doves of peace athwart the breeze.
The multitude arising in the spiral of the hymn.

Now, at night, joy has
official outlines.

The city is decked out
with jubilant billboards.

The dark fish of the Island has
glowing scales.

Words hang from buildings:
Peace. Future. Jobs.

The factories on sidewalks display
big blackboards with production figures.

Girls without makeup guard show windows
while rifles eclipse their breasts.

The "comrade" organizers
tour foreigners through the map,

in a perfect order
of visits and applause.

Peace! Future! Jobs!

The city laughs face upward
under a crust of light.

The wee hours crawl by.
Silence sets its sails.

Tropical winds drag together
dead words and paper litter.

A visitor of gloom descends
upon concrete and asphalt dumb.

And in the sordid dungeon
against a wall of fright,

as if a tunnel of hate spewed
its hidden lava,

a youth falls to the firing squad
and dies, pure, in his corner of Freedom.

Alejandro Almanza

Una Noche, Cuba 1963

Bajo la noche de aguas ancestrales
se extiende la ciudad.

Trópico de altos peces
y piel de sol.

Escenario de eléctricas agujas,
la Isla es el testimonio que arde y crece.

Cuba aquí, entre banderas,
estremecida de himnos y de escamas.

A maquillaje gris, a polvo denso,
la ciudad tiene un rostro formidable.

En el día irrumpieron los desfiles
de cañón en reposo y bala atenta.

Hombres de frentes graves
con mirada geométrica, marchaban.

Caminaba la risa de los niños
como trigo meciéndose entre filas.

Todo era animación de sindicatos,
oleadas de carteles y sones de consignas.

Palomas blancas, con la Paz, al viento.
La multitud subiendo por la espiral del himno.

Ahora, en la noche, la alegría tiene
oficiales contornos.

Con carteles de júbilo
la ciudad se atavía.

El pez oscuro de la Isla tiene
escamas encendidas.

Cuelgan palabras por los edificios:
Paz. Futuro. Trabajo.

Las fábricas sacaron a la acera
grandes pizarras con sus estadísticas.

Muchachas sin cosméticos custodian las vidrieras
mientras el rifle les eclipsa el seno.

Los "compañeros" organizadores
llevan los extranjeros por el mapa,

con un orden perfecto
de visitas y aplausos.

¡Paz! ¡Futuro! ¡Trabajo!

La ciudad ríe boca arriba
con corteza de luz.

Crece la madrugada.
La quietud ancla su velamen.

El viento de los trópicos arrastra
palabras muertas y papeles juntos.

Un visitante lúgubre desciende
sobre el cemento y el asfalto mudos.

y en la mazmorra sórdida
contra un muro de espanto,

como si un túnel de odio vomitase
su lava oculta,

un joven cae fusilado y puro
y muere en su rincón la Libertad.

Alejandro Almanza

Now the Swarms and Flocks Are Superfluous

Now the swarms and flocks are superfluous.
Now they call the fatherland: communism.
Man is little more than a dried brick;
Even children are made to sing hymns to war.
Those on top betray their preachments
and push the Island to self-destruct.
Words are distributed by the thousands
while bread is a lie not in short supply.
The poor are still poor and limited
to empty slogans in their pockets.
Now the Apostle of Cuba is no longer Martí:
Marx and Lenin have seen to that.
For any reason at all the beehive is aroused,
allowing the few to suck up the honey.
Meantime, the sun fights and vies
to give back its light to the crocodile.*
                                            Remigio Palma

Ahora el Enjambre y Los Rebaños Sobran

Ahora el enjambre y los rebaños sobran,
le llaman a la Patria: comunismo.
El hombre es un ladrillo más que seco;
hacen cantar la guerra hasta a los niños.
Los de arriba desdicen de sus prédicas
y empujan a la Isla hasta el suicidio.
Reparten a millares las palabras
y el pan es un engaño repetido.
El pobre sigue pobre y limitado,

---

*Because of its shape, Cuba is often pictured as a crocodile.

tan sólo con consigna en sus bolsillos.
Ya el Apóstol de Cuba no es Martí:
entre Marx y Lenín se la han cogido.
Por todo a la colmena la alborotan
y chupan de la miel unos poquitos.
El sol, en tanto, lucha y se debate
por devolver su luz al cocodrilo.

                                    Remigio Palma

[Editing and translations in the preceding chapter by Warren Hampton.]

From the Preface to Angel Cuadra's
Book of Poetry *Tiempo del hombre* (1977)

. . . Dusting off so many memorable dates, I behold streets, dreams, old songs shared with him. Exact facts I cannot offer you. Everything about my poet friend becomes an emotional reminiscence. I can simply tell you of seeing him receive, of a pleasant afternoon in the Aula Magna at the University, the Rubén Martínez Villena prize for his *Canto de amor al alma mater*. I can also recall youthful soirées at students' and writers' homes when he was the moving spirit of the literary group Renuevo.

I can picture him still in his athlete's togs, full of vigor and muscular good looks, when he was a member of the University track team, shouldering his trophies with the same modest grace as when draping himself with a fresh towel. I can tell of the illusion of rehearsal evenings; of the noctivagant hot chocolate in a Belascoaín street café while we all chattered over the play we were staging; remark his moments of triumph at the University Theater and on other stages; the trips with the Patronato del Teatro, the dances, serenades, *tertulias*, excursions—in the zestful ambiance of stage life.

I can embrace him once more, as when he got his law degree and opened his office, bearing with pride the title "doctor" while wreathed in a smile of affection.

I can suffer the years of civil strife, when he and I spoke for a Revolution we believed democratic; recall his rebel verses . . . which in the year we dreamt of liberty were collected into his book *Peldaño*. Once more can I be with him and his sweetheart

Pura del Prado, Cuadra's trusted friend during the revolutionary years, as a University of Havana student in the mid-1950s.

Elisa, can I demand of the clock all the impetuous joy they robbed him of.

I wish there were space to speak of Angel as one should, down to the bitter dregs of his disillusion and indignation; to reproduce herein the beautiful letters he has written me during his years as a fighter and prisoner so you could marvel at his soul; so you could love him as I do, with the devotion, respect and admiration of his heroic being. I wish I could sculpt him as he is: Christian, generous, clean, self-sacrificing, valiant, good; refer to this sweet man, so manly in thought, passions and ideals. But not even that, nor so much more that I should want to transmit can be enclosed in a modest preface. But, as a poet, Angel Cuadra needs it not; his verse stands out best when traveling alone, naked.

. . . He is a political prisoner unsurpassed in patriotic idealism, nor does he hate. . . . The government of Peru awarded him a prize for a poem. Prison bars have not prevented his being honored for the talent he carries in his head. Angel is more than a poet; he is poetic fire transmuted into conduct. No prison cell exists that could repress his verse. . . .

                                                              Pura del Prado

[Translation by Warren Hampton.]